FAR FROM THE M~~ADDING CROWD~~
BY THOMAS HARDY

MACMILLAN MASTER GUIDES

General Editor: James Gibson

Published:
JANE AUSTEN: **PRIDE AND PREJUDICE** Raymond Wilson
EMMA Norman Page
MANSFIELD PARK Richard Wirdnam
ROBERT BOLT: **A MAN FOR ALL SEASONS** Leonard Smith
EMILY BRONTË: **WUTHERING HEIGHTS** Hilda D. Spear
GEOFFREY CHAUCER: **THE PROLOGUE TO THE CANTERBURY TALES** Nigel Thomas and Richard Swan
CHARLES DICKENS: **GREAT EXPECTATIONS** Dennis Butts
HARD TIMES Norman Page
GEORGE ELIOT: **MIDDLEMARCH** Graham Handley
SILAS MARNER Graham Handley
OLIVER GOLDSMITH: **SHE STOOPS TO CONQUER** Paul Ranger
THOMAS HARDY: **FAR FROM THE MADDING CROWD** Colin Temblett-Wood
CHRISTOPHER MARLOWE: **DOCTOR FAUSTUS** David A. Male
GEORGE ORWELL: **ANIMAL FARM** Jean Armstrong
WILLIAM SHAKESPEARE: **MACBETH** David Elloway
A MIDSUMMER NIGHT'S DREAM Kenneth Pickering
ROMEO AND JULIET Helen Morris
THE WINTER'S TALE Diana Devlin

Forthcoming:
GEOFFREY CHAUCER: **THE MILLER'S TALE** Michael Alexander
T. S. ELIOT: **MURDER IN THE CATHEDRAL** Paul Lapworth
E. M. FORSTER: **A PASSAGE TO INDIA** Hilda D. Spear
WILLIAM GOLDING: **THE SPIRE** Rosemary Sumner
THOMAS HARDY: **TESS OF THE D'URBERVILLES** James Gibson
HARPER LEE: **TO KILL A MOCKINGBIRD** Jean Armstrong
ARTHUR MILLER: **THE CRUCIBLE** Leonard Smith
GEORGE BERNARD SHAW **ST JOAN** Leonee Ormond
WILLIAM SHAKESPEARE: **HAMLET** Jean Brooks
HENRY IV PART ONE Helen Morris
JULIUS CAESAR David Elloway
KING LEAR Francis Casey
OTHELLO Christopher Beddowes
TWELFTH NIGHT Edward Leeson
RICHARD SHERIDAN: **THE RIVALS** Jeremy Rowe
THE SCHOOL FOR SCANDAL Paul Ranger
JOHN WEBSTER: **THE DUCHESS OF MALFI/THE WHITE DEVIL** David A. Male
THE METAPHYSICAL POETS Joan van Emden

Also published by Macmillan

MACMILLAN MASTER SERIES

Mastering English Literature R. Gill
Mastering English Language S. H. Burton
Mastering English Grammar S. H. Burton

MACMILLAN MASTER GUIDES

FAR FROM THE MADDING CROWD BY THOMAS HARDY

COLIN TEMBLETT-WOOD

MACMILLAN

First edition 1985

Published by
MACMILLAN EDUCATION LTD
Houndmills, Basingstoke, Hampshire RG21 2XS
and London
Companies and representatives
throughout the world

Printed in Hong Kong

British Library Cataloguing in Publication Data
Temblett-Wood, Colin
Far from the madding crowd by Thomas Hardy. —
(Macmillan master guides)
1. Hardy, Thomas, *1840–1928*. Far from the
madding crowd
I. Title
823'.8   PR4745
ISBN 0-333-37434-7 Pbk
ISBN 0-333-39465-8 Pbk export

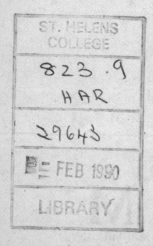

CONTENTS

ACKNOWLEDGEMENTS

Cover illustration: *Glowed with Tints of Evening Hours* by Joseph Farquharson. © Roy Miles Fine Paintings, London, courtesy of the Bridgeman Art Library.

GENERAL EDITOR'S PREFACE

The aim of the Macmillan Master Guides is to help you to appreciate the book you are studying by providing information about it and by suggesting ways of reading and thinking about it which will lead to a fuller understanding. The section on the writer's life and background has been designed to illustrate those aspects of the writer's life which have influenced the work, and to place it in its personal and literary context. The summaries and critical commentary are of special importance in that each brief summary of the action is followed by an examination of the significant critical points. The space which might have been given to repetitive explanatory notes has been devoted to a detailed analysis of the kind of passage which might confront you in an examination. Literary criticism is concerned with both the broader aspects of the work being studied and with its detail. The ideas which meet us in reading a great work of literature, and their relevance to us today, are an essential part of our study, and our Guides look at the thought of their subject in some detail. But just as essential is the craft with which the writer has constructed his work of art, and this is considered under several technical headings – characterisation, language, style and stagecraft.

The authors of these Guides are all teachers and writers of wide experience, and they have chosen to write about books they admire and know well in the belief that they can communicate their admiration to you. But you yourself must read and know intimately the book you are studying. No one can do that for you. You should see this book as a lamppost. Use it to shed light, not to lean against. If you know your text and know what it is saying about life, and how it says it, then you will enjoy it, and there is no better way of passing an examination in literature.

JAMES GIBSON

1 LIFE AND BACKGROUND

Thomas Hardy was born and brought up, went to school, worked as architect and as writer in the county of Dorset, which was to be the main setting for his novels. He also lived in London; he met his first wife while working in Cornwall. But Dorset was the centre of his life and his writing. Even when he was an old man and internationally famous, he still looked the countryman. Another novelist, Somerset Maugham, described him like this:

> I remember a little man with an earthy face. In his evening
> clothes, with his boiled shirt and high collar, he had still
> a strange look of the soil.

1.1 EARLY DAYS

His parents were Dorset people. Both his father and grandfather were small builder masons; his great-grandfather built a cottage in the hamlet of Higher Bockhampton near Dorchester, the county town of Dorset. Here Hardy was born in 1840, here he spent his childhood, here he wrote *Far from the Madding Crowd*. His mother's family also was local, many of her relatives living in Puddletown, the 'Weatherbury' of the novel, only two miles from Hardy's home. Hardy was related to a network of families as his mother was one of seven children, his father one of six. It was said that one of his uncles on his mother's side was the model for Sergeant Troy in *Far from the Madding Crowd*.

As a child he listened to many local tales and legends especially those told by his grandmother and his mother both of whom had a fund of fascinating stories. These must have increased his delight in the heath and woodlands round his home and enlivened his Sunday walks with his parents. However, they also horrified him: stories of hangings and suicides and brutalities that were a part of local history haunted him all his life. Episodes such as Fanny Robin's death owe their macabre intensity to this sensitivity of the young Hardy, who, even as a child, was acutely conscious of the horror and suffering life can bring.

His mother encouraged his reading and was anxious that he should benefit as fully as possible from his schooling, arranging for him to take Latin as an extra. His father was supportive in this and, as his business was doing well at the time, was able to afford the fees for a private education when Hardy's teacher, Issac Last, set up his own school in Dorchester in 1853. His father was an able musician and taught Hardy the violin which became something of an obsession with him in adolescence. Playing at weddings and dances helped to widen the young man's awareness of country traditions and junketings. These could be boisterous; perhaps the scene in the barn when Troy takes over the harvest festivities reflects some memories of these occasions.

1.2 THE APPRENTICE ARCHITECT

Just after his sixteenth birthday Hardy became apprenticed to a local architect, John Hicks of Dorchester, whom his father had met while working as a mason. Hicks was an educated, well-read man who encouraged his apprentices to pursue their own reading and also joined with them in general discussions. Hardy was to continue working as an architect when he moved to London in 1862 and again in 1867 when he returned to Dorset to rejoin Hicks. His architectural knowledge is particularly evident in *Far from the Madding Crowd* in which buildings, especially the Great Barn, are significant features of the story's setting.

A friendship he had formed in Dorset with a brilliant and widely-read clergyman, Horace Moule, had stimulated Hardy to widen his intellectual horizons, and while practising as an architect in London he took the opportunities the city offered to extend his knowledge of the arts, particularly painting; he also read extensively, studying anthologies of great writers. His deep knowledge of literature and the range of his reading is evident in all his writing – though sometimes it can be self-conscious.

While in London he started to write poetry and also a novel. Although this was not accepted for publication he was encouraged to try again and by 1870 had completed a second work, *Desperate Remedies*, which was published in 1871.

1.3 *FAR FROM THE MADDING CROWD*

By the summer of 1873 he had returned to Dorset and started work on *Far from the Madding Crowd*. In the familiar security of his own home, drawing on the inspiration which the people and landscape of the area provided, Hardy wrote the novel under particularly favourable conditions. The first instalment was published in the *Cornhill Magazine* in January 1874 and favourable reviews soon followed

Hardy was now an established author; the book was beginning to sell well in America as well as in this country. The consequent promise of financial security may have helped fix the date for his marriage to Emma Gifford in September 1874. *Far from the Madding Crowd* appeared in book form in November and was well received; the first edition of 1000 copies had sold out by January 1875.

He now gave up his architectural work and turned wholly to writing. His later novels, especially *Tess of the d'Urbervilles* and *Jude the Obscure* offended a large section of the Victorian reading public largely because of what was then considered a shockingly frank treatment of sexual matters. Hardy was distressed by this reaction and after the storm of abuse that greeted *Jude the Obscure* on its publication in 1895 (one reviewer gasping that he could hardly imagine a book 'more disgusting, more impious as regards human nature, more foul in detail') he decided to write no more novels but concentrate on what had been his first love: poetry.

By this time he had designed his own house at Dorchester, Max Gate, where he continued to write poetry. His marriage to Emma drifted into a sadly cold and distant relationship, their interests and temperaments moving further and further apart until her death in 1912. This released in him a flood of memories of their early happy days which he recorded in a series of poems of moving power. He married again two years later.

He continued to publish poetry. His stature as a writer was increasingly recognised: he was awarded the Order of Merit in 1910 and honorary degrees by the universities of St Andrews, Aberdeen, Bristol, Oxford and Cambridge. Other writers and admirers called constantly at Max Gate. A collection of poems published in 1925 in an edition of 5000 copies was sold out almost before publication.

His heart was buried in Stinsford Churchyard beside his family's graves; his ashes were placed in Westminster Abbey in January 1928, the service being attended by the Prime Minister of the day and a host of distinguished persons.

2 SUMMARIES AND CRITICAL COMMENTARY

Chapter 1

Gabriel Oak is presented; he watches a young girl perched on a waggon loaded with household goods, then pays the toll (a charge which used to be made for travelling along a road) that she had thought excessive.

This first chapter presents a static 'portrait': we are given information and description over three pages before any action takes place. Does this seem to you slow and clumsy? Or does it lend a solidity and firmness to the opening of the novel – very appropriate to Oak himself?

The whole story is to involve deep passions, betrayal, tragedy, death, but there is no hint of any of these here. The very first sentence describes Gabriel's smile and the whole character of the writing in this and in the next three chapters is playful, a kind of romantic comedy: awkward lover meets girl who plays hard to get.

Gabriel is described as 'Farmer Oak': we have a sense of his being superior in status to the girl. He also helps her over a difficulty by paying the toll. This is a gentle way of hinting at the essence of their relationship: time and again he will intervene to rescue Bathsheba from a tricky situation.

Chapter 2

Oak, attending at night to his lambing ewes, sees an unfamiliar light. He goes towards it and finds it comes from a low shed tucked under a slope. Spying through a crack in the roof he watches two women tending a cow that has calved; one of them he recognises as the girl on the waggon.

The realities of farming life, so important to the whole fabric of the novel, are introduced: we are told that Oak has had to work hard for a year to lease and stock his small sheepfarm and still owes money for his flock; Bathsheba wishes she and her aunt could afford to pay a man to help them.

Also we have the first example of the kind of close observation that is one of the hallmarks of Hardy's writing. Both precise and poetic, this sort of detail gives a sense of reality to the world in which his story exists:

> The thin grasses, more or less coating the hill, were touched by the wind in breezes of differing powers, and almost of different natures - one rubbing the blades heavily, another raking them piercingly, another brushing them like a soft broom.

Chapter 3

The next morning Gabriel watches Bathsheba searching for her hat which had blown away the previous night. He finds it and returns it to her; she is embarrassed to learn he had been watching her. Five days later Gabriel overheats the stove in his shepherd's hut and might have suffocated had not his dog alerted Bathsheba, who comes to his rescue.

In spite of the fact that Gabriel nearly dies of suffocation, the tone of this chapter is not really dramatic; the incident is made light of as the relationship between Gabriel and Bathsheba grows in a warm and teasingly comic manner. Also the fact that Gabriel probably owes his life to Bathsheba is not in any way insisted on as the story develops.

Chapter 4

Gabriel finds an excuse to call on Bathsheba and asks her to marry him. She turns him down.

This proposal and its rejection are described in a light-hearted way: a young shepherd, naïvely and clumsily sure that he will be accepted, is baffled by a spirited country girl who has no intention of getting involved with him. Gabriel's elaborate preparations with new boot-straps, walking-stick and handkerchief, an elegant waistcoat and lashings of hair-oil are all a touch absurdly self-conscious. It is also comic when, on being told that Bathsheba has a dozen young men after her, Gabriel promptly ups and leaves. He is not a very determined lover at this moment, even admitting to Bathsheba that he really ought to marry someone with money. In fact, we are given no sense as yet of the deep seriousness and commitment of Gabriel's love.

Chapter 5

Bathsheba inherits her uncle's farm at Weatherbury and Gabriel loses all his sheep which are chased over the cliff edge by an untrained young sheepdog.

So two highly significant events occur simultaneously; they swing the story into a new and quite unexpected direction. Here we have a complete reversal of roles and status: Gabriel is reduced to the rank of a farm-labourer, a hired hand; Bathsheba becomes a woman of property, an employer.

It might be said that these twin dramatic and totally chance events are clumsy devices, invented to jerk the story forward. But do they strike you in this way? After all, sudden changes of fortune do in life often distort people's situations.

Chapter 6

Oak, still looking for employment, fails to be offered a job at the hiring fair at Casterbridge. He decides to try again at Shotsford, as this town is very close to the farm Bathsheba now owns. On his way there he passes her farm, sees a rick on fire and helps to put it out. He meets Bathsheba and asks her for a job.

More coincidences: acceptable? or straining the reader's sense of probability? This is another of the occasions when Gabriel is of vital assistance to Bathsheba, and also the first of several vividly dramatic night scenes which are to be so effective in the novel.

Chapter 7

Gabriel is taken on as a shepherd by Bathsheba. Later he meets a girl in the churchyard who asks him not to say that he has seen her. (We do not know at this point that she is Fanny Robin, leaving the village to hold Troy to his promise of marriage.)

The opening phase of the story is here completed: Gabriel is now in Bathsheba's employment; until the very end of the novel he is to remain close to her but yet separated - lover and servant. Fanny is a pre-echo of the tragedies to come.

The tension is subtly adjusted in this chapter: another night scene, a chilling churchyard setting, an unexplained and unnamed figure introduced: 'the motionless stranger'. A key phrase sets a tone we have not yet heard: 'a throb of tragic intensity'.

Chapter 8

At the malthouse Gabriel meets the old maltster with other local characters. Local gossip is interrupted by news of two startling events: the dismissal of Pennyways, Bathsheba's bailiff, for stealing the disappearance of Fanny Robin.

The folk who gather at the malthouse are of much importance even though they rarely affect the course of the story. Their simplicity, shrewdness and good nature are to counterpoint the dramatic happenings of the main narrative. The scene has a warmth and geniality that radiate through the whole novel, even though tragic events are to follow. While the work-folk are certainly comic, their conversation rich with unconscious humour, they also have an innocence and spirit of good fellowship that make us warm to them. The God-forgive-me circulates freely, Gabriel is offered the gritty bacon, and his flute-playing is well-received largely because he plays 'merry tunes' and not bawdy songs. Christian precepts and notions of proper behaviour figure prominently in these God-fearing folk's judgements.

Chapter 9

Bathsheba's neighbour, Boldwood, calls enquiring whether there is any news of Fanny Robin.

The detailed description of both the exterior and interior of Weatherbury Farm is a reminder both of Hardy's architectural training and of the import-ance of buildings in the story (this latter point is considered in the discussion of 'Wessex' in Chapter 3, 'Themes and Concerns'). Note also the introduction of Boldwood: it is done 'off-stage'; that is to say, we never see him, only hear his horse, his knock, his voice. His oddly formal enquiry about Bathsheba, 'She is a staid woman, isn't she . . .?' is given us at second-hand. The foreground is taken up, not by Boldwood, but by Liddy, Maryann Money, Mrs and Master Coggan, all of whom are sharply and entertainingly presented. A full account of Boldwood is delayed until chapter 18. Why do you think Hardy introduced a major character in this oblique way?

Chapter 10

Bathsheba announces she will not be appointing a new bailiff but will run the farm herself; she pays her work-people. News is brought that Fanny has a soldier as a lover and has followed him.

Comedy continues with Andrew Randle's stammer, the 'scarlet pair', Temperance and Soberness, Laban Tall's 'lawful wife'. However, the con-text here is not the social gossip and relaxation of the malthouse; this is a place of work, and the careful scrutiny Bathsheba gives to each employee shows her as a very competent manager.

Chapter 11

Fanny finds Troy at his barracks; he agrees to meet her the next day to arrange their wedding.

With this chapter the story enters a new phase. Although we have already glimpsed Fanny in chapter 7 and been given hints of her tragic isolation, this scene is grimly foreboding, the atmosphere dark, chill, bleak. The girl's figure below the looming barrack wall is so vulnerable, and whatever Frank promises, the final 'low peal of laughter' mocks the pathetic Fanny. What a dramatic change Hardy has already fashioned from the comedy of Gabriel's wooing and the close companionship of the maltster's gathering.

Chapter 12

Bathsheba goes to the cornmarket and is annoyed that Boldwood ignores her.

Hardy is carefully moving his story forward: Fanny and Troy have been brought together (though we sense an uneasiness in their situation); now the relationship between Bathsheba and Boldwood is gently nudged along. Again Boldwood is presented obliquely in that we don't know (though we may well guess) the identity of the man of dignity who takes no notice of Bathsheba. One effect of this approach is to make the reader share Bathsheba's experience: like her, we are puzzled and irritated.

Chapter 13

Bathsheba impulsively decides to send Boldwood a valentine.

A great deal of the development of the story has its source in this trivial incident and you may feel that too much is made to depend on it. Remember, however, that Boldwood is an unusual type: Bathsheba has no sense of the force of passion locked in him; and she is smarting from his indifference to her. The collision now set in motion has its real source in the personalities of the two people concerned.

Chapter 14

Boldwood is fascinated by the valentine.

The way in which the aloof bachelor reacts so strongly is given a particular intensity: 'the large red seal became a blot on the retina of his eye'; he puts it on the corner of the looking-glass in his bedroom where the tantalising message stares back at him in the moonlight 'a pale sheen . . . lighting up the ceiling' in 'an unnatural way' and haunts him all night. This kind of unusual but precise and arresting detail is very characteristic of Hardy.

Chapter 15

Oak receives a letter from Fanny telling him of her forthcoming marriage. Boldwood asks Gabriel to identify the handwriting on the envelope in which the valentine had been sent and learns that it came from Bathsheba.

Before Boldwood is introduced in this chapter there is another delightful scene at the malthouse which has the same leisurely comedy of chapter 8, but with the addition of Gabriel's new-born lambs. So in one episode we have an unobtrusively skilful counterpointing of key elements in the story: the workfolk discussing their mistress, Gabriel as shepherd and as preserver of life, Boldwood's interest in Bathsheba and Fanny Robin's involvement with Troy.

Chapter 16

Fanny mistakes Troy's directions and goes to the wrong church; so the marriage does not take place.

Yet another chance event is to prove of major importance: had this marriage taken place, then Bathsheba and Troy could not have been married. In a very brief chapter, this significant episode is related almost curtly, as if to reflect Troy's hurt pride at being exposed to the titters and giggling in the church. That Troy should not commit himself to a repetition of the experience is less surprising than his ever agreeing to marry Fanny in the first place. His continuing love for her is perhaps the most interesting aspect of his character.

Chapter 17

At the cornmarket Boldwood finds himself jealously attracted to Bathsheba and she is aware of his interest.

In a different way, another key moment is also very briefly described. The importance here is not, as in chapter 16, in an event but in the development of the relationship between two major characters. For Boldwood, 'His heart began to move within him'; and for Bathsheba comes the realisation of the full embarrassment of her position: if she apologises for the valentine she will either offend Boldwood or make him think her a flirt. Yet the tone of this chapter is still light, even comic, with Boldwood, for instance, having to consult a neighbour to find out whether Bathsheba is considered a beautiful woman. A hint of the violence to come is reserved for the next chapter.

Chapter 18

Boldwood watches Bathsheba on the fields of her farm. He first resolves to speak to her, then changes his mind.

This chapter gives us important comment on Boldwood: his seriousness; the way in which his apparently finely balanced and controlled personality has been violently wrenched and is now 'a hotbed of tropic intensity'. Bathsheba also begins to realise the existence of that 'hotbed' and deeply regrets that she has stirred his emotions by the frivolous valentine.

Chapter 19

At the sheep-dipping Boldwood proposes to Bathsheba, who refuses him, but reluctantly gives permission for him to ask again at some future date.

So characteristically of the novel, a moment of high passion is set against the physical realities of country life seen as part of the year's cycle. It is May, lush with growth: 'every flower that was not a buttercup was a daisy'; the leaves are 'new, soft and moist'. A sharply effective detail describes Boldwood's boots 'which the yellow pollen from the buttercups had bronzed'. Traditionally the time for love to throb, there is a stiffness and irony in this May scene of lovers meeting.

It has often been noted that the sequence of the sheep-farmer's yearly concerns is carefully placed throughout the novel. We have already had the winter lambing; now the dipping of the sheep is accurately and vividly presented.

Chapter 20

Bathsheba asks Oak what the men are saying about her and Boldwood and what Gabriel's own opinion is of her conduct. Annoyed by his frank comments she orders him to leave the farm.

Another detail of a shepherd's working life is here used to ironic purpose: Gabriel is sharpening the shears in preparation for the sheep-shearing and Bathsheba tries to help, but she is clumsy; Gabriel has to tell her:

> 'You don't hold the shears right, miss – I knew you wouldn't know the way – hold like this.'
> He relinquished the winch, and enclosing her two hands completely in his own (taking each as we sometimes clasp a child's hand in teaching him to write), grasped the shears with her. 'Incline the edge so,' he said.
> Hands and shears were inclined to suit the words, and held thus for a peculiarly long time by the instructor as he spoke.
> 'That will do,' exclaimed Bathsheba. 'Loose my hands. I won't have them held! Turn the winch.'
> Gabriel freed her hands quietly, retired to his handle and the grinding went on.

It's a lovely moment. Try to work out for yourself the contrasting aspects of Gabriel's and Bathsheba's relationship suggested here. Or imagine you are directing an actor and actress rehearsing for a film version: what suggestions would you make about how they should look at each other, touch each other, to bring out on camera everything hinted at in the text?

Chapter 21

Bathsheba's sheep stray into a clover field and are 'blasted' (swollen in the stomach through eating the clover). Only Gabriel has the skill to save them, so Bathsheba is forced to appeal for his help. After making her ask him in a civil and humble manner Gabriel treats the sheep. Bathsheba reinstates him.

Bathsheba's dependence on Gabriel and his loyalty to her are once again emphasised. The incident is in part serious with the suffering of the sheep and the very damaging consequences for Bathsheba were they to be lost, in part comic with the farmhands' panic and helplessness, Bathsheba being forced to eat humble pie. The balance is finely adjusted so that we enjoy the humour, share the threat of disaster and surely are happy to see Gabriel no longer at the mercy of Bathsheba's whims.

Chapter 22

At the sheep-shearing Boldwood speaks privately to Bathsheba – making Gabriel uncomfortable.

The description of the great barn where the shearing takes place is a key reference-point for a major theme of the novel: the value of a steady continuity of community life. This is discussed later in Chapter 3, 'Themes and Concerns'.

Chapter 23

At the sheep-shearing supper Boldwood again presses Bathsheba for an answer; she promises to make up her mind by harvest time.

Another event of the 'country calendar'. The detail of the scene is interesting and revealing.

First – the seating arrangements. The table is set so that the workfolk are outside the house, Bathsheba inside with Gabriel opposite in a place of importance but still not inside the house and also some distance from her. Later he has to give up his place to Boldwood – who in due course moves inside the house to be with Bathsheba.

Second – the songs. Look at the words. What sort of reference does each song make indirectly to the central situations of the story?

In this scene the main characters (for even Troy is suggested as you will have spotted if you looked at the songs carefully) are all placed in a particular relationship. The scene is both tenderly and menacingly suggestive.

Chapter 24

Bathsheba literally bumps into Troy; his spur becomes entangled in her dress; he flirts with her while disengaging it.

At the end of chapter 23 the central situation has reached a moment of poised suspension. If we ask: 'What is going to happen now?' we can see no clear answer beyond the not very exciting prospect of how Bathsheba will cope with Boldwood when harvest comes. Clearly a fresh thrust and momentum is needed at this point. Troy has been held waiting in the wings for just this purpose.

The drama of their encounter is sharply rendered – in yet another night scene:

> A hand seized the lantern, the door was opened, the rays burst out from their prison, and Bathsheba beheld her position with astonishment.
>
> The man to whom she was hooked was brilliant in brass and scarlet. He was a soldier. His sudden appearance was to darkness what the sound of a trumpet is to silence.

The obvious symbolism of her being literally hooked by Troy speaks for itself.

Chapter 25

A further lengthy set portrait, this time of Troy. He meets Bathsheba in her hayfields.

Our knowledge of Troy is extended by this passage. However, it has been said that Hardy is not too successful in handling this type of character (the swashbuckling seducer). You may sense a certain ponderousness, too deliberate an approach almost as if Hardy did not trust his narrative to reveal the man convincingly. Certainly Hardy's style here is at times laborious. This sentence, for example, is pretty heavy-going:

> Nevertheless, that a male dissembler who by deluging her with untenable fictions charms the female wisely, may acquire powers reaching to the extremity of perdition, is a truth taught to many by unsought and wringing occurrences.

Chapter 26

Troy flirts with Bathsheba and tries to make her accept his father's gold watch.

A critical scene. Troy begins just flirting with a pretty woman and his declaration that he loves her is no more than his usual casual technique. But her agitation, so that she stands 'excited, wild and honest as the day' *does* begin to make him fall in love. The flirtation suddenly becomes a more serious game. As for Bathsheba, how can she resist a handsome soldier who tells her to her face that she is beautiful and then presses on her a watch having a direct association with his romantically noble illegitimacy?

Chapter 27

Troy hives a swarm of bees; he invites Bathsheba to a display of sword-exercise. She accepts.

In this and in the previous chapter there is a deft balance of comedy and growing passion which echoes Gabriel's advances to Bathsheba at the opening of the story. The way in which comedy, country wooing, strength of feeling and tragic complication are blended and balanced is one of the major achievements of the novel.

Chapter 28

Troy dazzles Bathsheba with his sword-play.

The whole episode has a boldness of invention and brilliance of detail that show Hardy at his best. Also, throughout the scene there are implications of a violent sexuality.

At the very opening the bracken is 'plump' and 'radiant'; the sun, a vigorously masculine 'bristling ball of gold', suggestively 'swept the tips of the ferns with its long, luxuriant rays'. Then Bathsheba runs to meet Troy: 'She was now literally trembling and panting . . . her breath came and went quickly.' The saucer-shaped hollow in which they met 'was floored with a thick flossy carpet of moss and grass intermingled, so yielding that the foot was half-buried within it'.

Troy's sword-play is excitingly dangerous: his blade catches the beams of the setting sun and dazzles her: 'she was enclosed in a firmament of light'.

Two final gestures by Troy are sexually provocative: he slices off a lock of her hair, then spears a caterpillar: 'She saw the point glisten towards her bosom and seemingly enter it. Bathsheba closed her eyes.' The climax is the kiss which 'set her stinging as if aflame to the very hollows of her feet'.

The reticence which Victorian public taste demanded in regard to sexual matters could be bypassed by a writer who knew how to write suggestively and to use imagery to powerfully subtle effect.

Chapter 29

Gabriel, deeply worried by what he has seen and sensed of Troy's advances to Bathsheba, warns her of the sergeant's bad reputation and tries to steer her back towards Boldwood – but without any success.

Three important aspects of the characters concerned are given emphasis at the opening of the chapter. Hardy comments on Bathsheba's inexperience, how she has no terms of reference outside the honest customs of Weatherbury and cannot detect (even had she wished to) Troy's essential flippancy. Even a woman of greater caution might have been deceived since, as we are reminded by Hardy, 'Troy's deformities lay deep down from a woman's view'. The contrast with Oak is made immediately: Gabriel's faults are hidden from no one, his qualities lie deep within him. This is perhaps the most selfless moment in his relationship with Bathsheba: disregarding his own love for her, his only concern is for her welfare.

Chapter 30

Bathsheba writes to Boldwood saying she cannot marry him and then tells her servant, Liddy, of her passionate love for Troy.

As a fine performance in the film version of *Far from the Madding Crowd* (directed by John Schlesinger, 1967) showed, Liddy is an interesting and touching characterisation although she has only a very minor role. This moving scene rings true and makes us the more concerned about the obvious dangers into which Bathsheba is rushing headlong.

Chapter 31

Out walking, Bathsheba meets Boldwood, who speaks wildly of the suffering her refusal is causing him. He knows Troy is after her and warns her to keep the sergeant away from him as he will not answer for the consequences should they meet.

This encounter is one of the worst experiences Bathsheba has to go through: deeply disturbed by this demonstration of the helpless violence of love in Boldwood, she has to face her own responsibility in arousing it and also the terror she feels over Boldwood's threats concerning Troy.

She is left 'beating the air with her fingers, pressing her brow, and sobbing brokenly to herself'.

The benign warmth of summer which has penetrated the recent episodes adjusts in mood to her tragic situation: 'Above the dark margin of the earth appeared foreshores and promontories of coppery cloud' (what splendid choice of words here) – which image the piling up of tragic circumstances as well as the great storm to come.

In this chapter the story takes another major shift in tone and seriousness.

Chapter 32

Gabriel and Jan Coggan are alerted to the fact that a horse and gig have been taken from the farm in the middle of the night. Suspecting a gipsy thief, they give chase but discover it is Bathsheba who is responsible. She sends them back and continues her impulsive journey to Bath to meet Troy and break off their relationship - that at least is her conscious intention.

This is the first (but not the only) moment in the story when Hardy keeps his reader pretty well in the dark about what is really happening, an effective device in increasing interest and tension.

A typically ironic touch is worth noting: Gabriel and Coggan take Boldwood's horses in their pursuit of Bathsheba.

Chapter 33

Bathsheba in Bath does not in fact reject Troy but marries him.

Hardy uses one of the workfolk, Cain Ball, to give an oblique account of Bathsheba's visit to Bath. The episode is deliberately comic; its effect is to prevent the story becoming too claustrophobically tragic. However grim the latter parts of the novel are to be, the final outcome is not unrelieved disaster and Hardy has skilfully made a slight adjustment in narrative technique here to keep in view a lighter perspective on the tragedies of passion and circumstance.

Chapter 34

Bathsheba returns with Troy to Weatherbury. Boldwood, not knowing of the marriage, but aware of Troy's relationship with Fanny, tries to buy Troy off, offering him money if he will leave Bathsheba. Troy jeeringly informs him of the marriage and throws back the money.

A fine scene of grim comedy. The contrast between the farmer's passionately obsessive devotion and Troy's truculent self-possession is dramatic. In fact the episode is almost written in dramatic form, the bulk of it being in dialogue.

The irony of the whole situation - which Troy exploits contemptuously - is particularly effective, as the reader is placed in Boldwood's situation, knowing nothing of the marriage until he, like Boldwood, reads the newspaper cutting.

An important detail is the way in which Fanny is reintroduced. Hardy needs to bring her back into focus now in preparation for the climactic scenes of her death.

Chapter 35

The next morning Troy greets Oak and Coggan, making clear that he is now master.

Immediately he is in part charge of the farm Troy is shown to be a destructive influence: he dislikes the old farmhouse and wants to modernise it, justifying his attitude by quoting a 'philosopher' who had told him,

'Creation and preservation don't do well together.' In everything he is to do on the farm Troy will disrupt that settled continuity of tradition that Weatherbury folk cherish.

Chapter 36

Troy has laid on a harvest supper in the great barn which he announces to be also a 'Wedding Feast'. Music, dancing and strong drink are provided; the women are sent home and in the ensuing 'jolly carouse' all the men become hopelessly drunk. Meanwhile a storm is threatening; Gabriel is concerned about the unprotected ricks and sets about covering them on his own.

In this and in the following chapters the storm is described with particular force and accuracy. In this chapter for example:

> in the sky dashes of buoyant cloud were sailing in a course at right angles to that of another stratum, neither of them in the direction of the breeze below. The moon, as seen through these films, had a lurid metallic look. The fields were sallow with the impure light, and all were tinged in monochrome, as if beheld through stained glass.

The toad in the path in front of Gabriel's cottage and the 'thin glistening streak' on the table inside left by a slug which had come indoors are further acutely observed details.

In other novels as well as in *Far from the Madding Crowd* Hardy uses a dramatic natural event in a central position to intensify the situation and to draw the characters into more intimate relationships.

Again we see Troy as disruptive: the great barn, of such significance as a centre of the ancient work-patterns of farming life, is here abused by the sergeant as a place of drunken revelry which threatens the whole harvest crop.

Chapter 37

Gabriel, with Bathsheba's help, covers the ricks during the height of the storm.

The description of the storm continues with observed detail that brings total conviction. During a lightning flash: 'A poplar in the immediate foreground was like an ink stroke on burnished tin.'

There is a matching precision in the relationship of Gabriel and Bathsheba:

> He felt a zephyr curling about his cheek, and turned. It was Bathsheba's breath – she had followed him, and was looking into the same chink.

Chapter 38

By morning Gabriel has covered all the stacks. Returning home he meets Boldwood and is astonished to learn that the love-crazed farmer has failed to protect any of his own ricks.

There are a series of telling contrasts in this chapter. First Gabriel, soaked and tired, suddenly realises that eight months before he had been putting out a fire at the same spot where he was now saving the ricks. He is nevertheless cheered by a sense of success in a good cause. Then Troy 'whistling' and the workfolk 'abashed' straggle out from the barn without so much as a glance at the ricks. The contrast with Gabriel is eloquent. Lastly, Boldwood, whose obsession with Bathsheba has led to the total neglect of his ricks, abandons his usual reserve and declares passionately to Gabriel, 'I am weak and foolish . . . I feel it is better to die than to live.'

Chapter 39

About six weeks after the storm Bathsheba and Troy, driving back from market, pass a woman on the road who speaks to Troy and then collapses. It is Fanny. Sending Bathsheba on, Troy speaks to her, gives her money and promises to meet her the next day. He pretends to Bathsheba that the girl was only a slight acquaintance.

It seems odd to us today that the demands of nineteenth-century public moral standards, particularly where the readership of influential lending libraries was concerned, prevented any indication at this point of Fanny's advanced pregnancy.

Chapter 40

Fanny struggles on to Casterbridge and is admitted to the workhouse where she is to die – presumably in giving birth to her stillborn child.

In describing at length Fanny's agonised progress to the workhouse and particularly in introducing a stray dog who befriends her and is then stoned away, Hardy may be thought to have made too deliberate an appeal to the reader's emotions. We know so little of Fanny, have seen her so seldom that this sudden account of her suffering may seem detached from the central flow of the story, rather like one of those moralising Victorian paintings – set pieces on somewhat sentimental topics.

However, this episode, has been much admired. James Gibson, editor of the Macmillan Students' Hardy edition of *Far from the Madding Crowd*, argues:

> There is a poetical and dramatic power present in this kind of writing which firmly links Hardy with Shakespeare. It is significant that not

once does Hardy refer to Fanny by name. She is the 'woman', and she stands out against the dark background of eternity as a symbol of *all* suffering women.

Make up your mind about your own reaction.

Chapter 41

Troy asks Bathsheba for money (which he intends to use to help Fanny) and reveals a lock of fair hair in his watch – Bathsheba's is dark. The next day he leaves the house early to meet Fanny (of course not knowing of her death). News of Fanny's death is then brought to Bathsheba, who connects the woman met on the road with the lock of hair, and becomes even more suspicious that Troy had been her lover.

A chapter of fast-rising pressures: the story is clearly approaching a climax. The bitterness of the conversation between Bathsheba and Troy is effectively placed as a prelude to crisis. A long paragraph in the middle of the chapter gives a moving account of Bathsheba's misery and interestingly emphasises her sexual morality: 'she had never, by look, word, or sign, encouraged a man to approach her' and she had even considered there to be a 'certain degradation' in a woman giving herself to a man in marriage. Ironically she has succumbed to a man about whom Gabriel had warned her, 'I believe him to have no conscience at all . . . Don't trust him.'

Chapter 42

Bathsheba arranges for Joseph Poorgrass to fetch Fanny's body so that it may be buried in Weatherbury Churchyard; but Joseph gets drunk and is so late in getting to the church that the burial has to be postponed. Bathsheba gives orders for the coffin to rest in her house overnight. Gabriel, ever protective, discreetly rubs out the damning words 'and child' from the chalked inscription.

This is the only time in the story when one of the workfolk is used as a vital element of the plot. Although the consequences of Joseph's drinking are fearsome, the incident itself is one of warm, delightful comedy, described at length and culminating in the gorgeous affliction of Joseph's 'multiplying eye'. Hardy's handling of the sequence shows a particularly sure touch in the dove-tailing of comedy into a tragic context. A richness of texture results, the kind of texture we associate with Shakespeare.

This chapter concluded the ninth instalment when the novel was originally published in serial form in the *Cornhill* magazine. It is a fine example of a theatrical conclusion with its revelation of Fanny's pregnancy and Oak's delicate concern for the woman he loves – and of course it leaves the reader panting to know what will happen in the next instalment.

Chapter 43

Bathsheba opens the coffin and sees the dead child. Troy, who has been vainly waiting for Fanny and is still ignorant of her death, returns. He kisses the dead Fanny and tells Bathsheba that Fanny meant everything to him. Bathsheba rushes out of the house.

Possibly the most tense and dramatic moment of the whole novel, this scene needed very careful handling to avoid tipping over into melodrama. There is admirable restraint in the writing, a firmness of control which allows the power of the situation to strike home with uncluttered directness. For example:

> 'Do you know her?' said Bathsheba in a small enclosed echo, as from the interior of a cell.
>
> 'I do,' said Troy.
>
> 'Is it she?'
>
> 'It is.'

Chapter 44

Bathsheba spends the night outside in a desolate hollow and is found in the morning by Liddy. They wait until Fanny's coffin is taken away, then return to the farmhouse where they retreat to an attic room dreading Troy's return.

It has been suggested that the hollow in which Bathsheba spends a terrible night is the same spot where Troy first dazzled her with his swordsmanship. This seems unlikely as there are references to rotting tree stumps, rushes and a swamp, none of which is appropriate to the original grassy stretch among the bracken. (Check on the detail in both descriptions and see what you think: the same or not?) Nevertheless, the place is described in detail: its listless, evil character certainly contrasts ironically with the golden glory of the previous hollow and is very expressive of the horror that Bathsheba has just experienced.

These eloquent images of decay are counterpointed in an unusual and striking way by two references to youngsters: first there is the passing schoolboy desperately learning the collect; then the boys playing Prisoners' base. This is the only time in the novel that there is a specific reference to children. The implication seems to be that life is renewed and vital even in the midst of desperate situations.

Chapter 45

Troy orders a tombstone for Fanny and plants flowers on her grave.

Troy's loyalty to Fanny and these final tributes to her, although in part the result of a guilty conscience, do affect our impression of him. However irresponsible and brutal he may have been to Bathsheba, there is no doubting the genuineness of his love for Fanny and his grief at her death.

Chapter 46

Troy's bulbs on Fanny's grave are washed away by the rainwater spouting from the church gargoyles. Bathsheba emerges from her attic hideout, goes to the churchyard, sees the inscription on Fanny's tomb, and replants Troy's plants and bulbs.

Perhaps the gargoyle is a less than subtle suggestion that a man's attempts at atonement for past wrongs are doomed to be swept aside by an indifferent universe. However, the sense of man as a tragic creature thwarted by hostile forces is not as insistently thrust on the reader as it is in some of Hardy's later novels

Chapter 47

Troy makes for the coast, swims out to sea and is caught by a fast current. Although he is rescued by a passing boat, his clothes have been left on the beach. Our knowing that Troy is still alive is important to the story's development as this creates suspense about his possible return.

This is the only time in the novel apart from the opening chapters when the reader is taken any distance from the environs of Weatherbury. The abrupt switch is dramatic in its very unusualness: 'a wide and novel prospect burst upon him'. It feels strange to us, as it does to Troy, to be looking at the 'broad steely sea' with its 'frill of milkwhite foam along the nearer angles of the shores'. However, this placid seascape is deceptive as the place has a 'sinister character'. The final description sets a vividly ominous mood as night falls and the lights of Budmouth gleam amid the 'thickening shades . . . each appearing to send a flaming sword deep down into the waves'.

Chapter 48

Troy's clothes are discovered by the coastguard; a witness, walking on the cliffs, testifies to having seen Troy carried out to sea. The obvious inference is that Troy has been drowned, and this news is brought to Bathsheba at the cornmarket. She faints and is rescued by Boldwood.

Some effective detail highlights Hardy's skill as a dramatic story-teller. There is Boldwood's brief ecstasy, 'those few heavenly, golden moments' when he carries Bathsheba in his arms, yet the possibilities this suggests are constrained by Bathsheba's inward conviction that Troy is still alive. Later she opens the watch and starts to burn Fanny's lock of hair. But at the last moment she snatches it back: 'No - I'll not burn it - I'll keep it in memory of her, poor thing!' How much this tells us of Bathsheba's essential generosity of spirit.

Chapter 49

Nine months pass. Distraught and secluded, both Bathsheba and Boldwood, unable to cope with their farms, appoint Oak as their bailiff. Boldwood nurses a hope that, as Troy is apparently dead, Bathsheba will eventually marry him.

It is important that Gabriel should now gradually be brought to the fore and promoted in status so as to be finally a fit partner for Bathsheba. Again he is shown as an active, positive influence: two farms are sustained through his determination and competence. Their owners are shown, in contrast, to be wholly withdrawn, Bathsheba in a state of 'general apathy' and Boldwood living only for a future hope: 'He would annihilate the six years of his life as if they were minutes - so little did he value his time on earth beside her love.'

Chapter 50

At the annual sheep fair at Greenhill an entertainment is put on by a troupe of performers. Troy is among them. After a spell in America he has returned and his skills as a horseman have found him a job with the company. Bathsheba, without recognising him, watches his performance; Troy, seeing her again, has thoughts of reclaiming her.

A lively and vigorous episode which serves to bring all the main characters together again as both Boldwood and Oak are also at the fair. The scene is visually dramatic and the film version of the novel saw its opportunities and re-created them excitingly.

Chapter 51

Escorting Bathsheba home from the fair Boldwood gets her to promise that she will tell him at Christmas whether she will eventually marry him. Later she asks Gabriel's advice about her promise; he advises her not to marry a man she does not love, but does not press his own claims - a reticence that secretly disappoints her.

The conversation between Bathsheba and Gabriel is carefully placed to keep him in the foreground. Without such preparation the ending of the novel might seem too sudden and unconvincing.

Chapter 52

Boldwood holds a Christmas Eve party whose secret purpose is to hold Bathsheba to her promise. Troy decides to take this opportunity to reclaim his wife.

This chapter is unique in the novel in that it is divided into sections. Hardy's technique here is essentially one of cross-cutting as used in the cinema, switching from one main character to another and back as each prepares for the party. The effect is to increase tension, giving a sense of separate characters each drawn irresistibly towards a common destiny.

Chapter 53

News has got around that Troy is in the neighbourhood and the farmhands try to warn Bathsheba, but without success. Boldwood detains Bathsheba, who very reluctantly agrees to marry him in six years' time. Troy joins the party and claims his wife. This is too much for Boldwood, who shoots him.

Again there is a deft use of the workfolk: comic in their well-meaning but ineffectual attempts to warn Bathsheba, they are not allowed to develop out of proportion or to undermine the drama of the situation. The climax is swift and as shatteringly unexpected to the reader as it is to those who witness it.

Chapter 54

Boldwood straightway gives himself up to the police. Bathsheba has Troy's body taken to her house where she lays it out for burial.

There is here a grandeur in the depiction of Bathsheba which marks the greatest remove from her first portrayal in the novel as a charming, winsome country girl. We are specifically told: 'As for Bathsheba, she had changed . . . astonishing all around her.' What causes the astonishment is her calm control: her 'quiet and simple words came with more force than a tragic declamation'. Her actions are even more impressive when she steels herself to dress Troy's body in its grave-clothes. She here rises to a tragic dignity that significantly strengthens her presentation as a character.

Chapter 55

Three months later Boldwood is tried and condemned to death, but a local petition results in the sentence being altered to life imprisonment on grounds of insanity.

It would be inappropriate to the 'pastoral tale' that *Far from the Madding Crowd* essentially is for Boldwood to be hanged. He is no villain,

has harmed no one except himself. A reprieve is therefore a fitting device.
But it is interesting to note that Boldwood is not a popular figure locally.
He has never fulfilled the role of squire nor patronised the local shop-
keepers, who are hence resentful and do not sign the petition.

Chapter 56

Months after Troy's death Bathsheba is still deeply affected and had left
all the management of the farm to Gabriel. When he gives in his notice
she calls him to discuss this and learns that he is only shunning local
gossip which has linked their names. Mutual misunderstandings are quickly
cleared up and their marriage agreed.

This relationship is founded on shared experience, not on passion.
The pair are not only lovers, but also comrades and fellow workers, an
intrinsic part of the Weatherbury community and of the values it cherishes.

Chapter 57

Gabriel and Bathsheba are married.

The final scene is left to the married couple – and to the workfolk.
It is fitting that it should be these humble people who celebrate with
Gabriel and Bathsheba: it is their world, their shared happiness.

3 THEMES AND CONCERNS

3.1 GENERAL THINKING

What is the meaning of the terms 'themes' and 'concerns' that head this section? How do they differ from 'plot' or 'story'?

If you ask someone what a novel (or a play or film also) is 'about' you will probably be given an outline of the story as an answer. In this sense *Far from the Madding Crowd* is 'about' a woman who is a country farmer and her relationships with three men. The storyline develops the relationships, the pressures they exert on Bathsheba and how she responds to these.

Although it is possible to construct novels without a strong narrative, Hardy always built his story up very firmly; the life of his novels is sustained by a backbone of closely linked episodes. (How he did this in *Far from the Madding Crowd* is discussed in the later Chapter 4, 'Technical Features'.)

Yet to say that *Far from the Madding Crowd* is a story is not the whole answer to the question, 'what is it about?' Any major novelist has his own sense of life: certain instincts and intuitions, ideas and values, which spring from his own experience and thinking. In writing a novel, part of his intention is to offer the reader his own convictions. He will use his characters and the situations in which he places them as his vocabulary of thought: the people, the incidents, the whole created world that the writer invents will express his ideas, his intellectual personality.

Think of a face, its features. In themselves these will tell us something about a person; but it is not really until the face is alive and expressive, showing warmth or fear, the eyes eager or the mouth sulky, that we are in contact with the reality of a person's response to life.

So it is with a novel. The set features of a face correspond to the essential features of a novel: the characters and their situation. The mobile and changing play of emotions across the features correspond to the expression of the writer's deepest feelings and thoughts which are revealed through the story and characters he presents. And just as you cannot separate an expression from a face – one cannot exist without the other – so one cannot isolate a novelist's ideas and themes and sense of values from the story and characters which embody them.

Therefore we can only detect Hardy's themes and concerns in *Far from the Madding Crowd* by looking carefully at what the story has to say.

3.2 'NOVELS OF CHARACTER AND ENVIRONMENT'

This phrase was used by Hardy to define the major group of his novels, including *Far from the Madding Crowd*. Let us think about these terms, taking 'character' first.

Without attempting a detailed consideration of individual characters (this is done in Chapter 4, 'Technical Features') can we see what kind of people Hardy is giving us? What do they suggest about his views on how personality is formed and developed, his sense of what is admirable or worthless in people?

Far from the Madding Crowd is essentially a love story. How do we react to the varied passions it presents?

Bathsheba's love

Bathsheba is swept off her feet by a misjudged infatuation. How do we feel about this?

In part we surely feel intense sympathy for what she had to go through. The teasing tomboyish girl we first see is torn by passion, suffers contemptuous rejection by the man she adores, bears courageously a traumatic experience. She has also to cope with unrelenting pressure from Boldwood.

Yet she asked for it. She flung herself at Troy (by going to Bath), disregarded the sound advice given her – and she provoked Boldwood by the valentine. However, she is also a victim, possessed by a daemon of love without the experience or resources to resist. Is this all her fault?

Such utter absorption is difficult to judge. How do we respond to any obsession that is clearly in some respects disastrous? For example, the explorer who feels compelled to set out on some dangerous, perhaps futile expedition, abandoning his family, sacrificing possibly his own life, even those of others. Heroic and splendid? Well, yes. Irresponsible and thoughtless? Yes, too. Or Shakespeare's Antony, ruthlessly sacrificing everything for an all-consuming love. Foolish? Clearly so. Magnificent? Surely.

However, such comparisons are no doubt misleading. Is Bathsheba really an heroic figure? Taken out of the full context of the story her conduct might be seen as heroic - stirring in its wild devotion of love whatever the price. Yet do we honestly think of her in this way? That is to say: does Hardy's theme here seem to be tragic grandeur and sacrifice for love?

Surely the answer must be: 'No, it doesn't feel like that. That isn't the way it comes across.' There are two main reasons for this reply.

The first is that Troy's death is not the end of the novel. (If it were, do you think we might have a different response to Bathsheba? If we left her after she had steeled herself to lay out her husband's corpse?) The end we have is, of course, the marriage to Gabriel, which is given us as the proper, the fitting, the admirable culmination of love. That suggests a very different set of values from any awed sense of the splendour of high romance and great passion.

The second reason is that the novel as a whole is just not conceived as tragic drama. It is a folk-tale set in a close-knit community of which Bathsheba is a vital component as farmer and employer. The point can best be made by a comparison with Hardy's later novel *Tess of the d'Urbervilles* where a woman's devotion *is* set in a grandly tragic context. Had Hardy been in a different frame of mind, less buoyant, when he wrote *Far from the Madding Crowd* it is conceivable that Bathsheba might have been the story of a somewhat thoughtless and passionate girl devastated by her own mistaken judgement. But that is not really what we have.

Bathsheba's relationships with both Troy and Boldwood are finally seen as passing episodes; the starting and the arrival points are Gabriel's patient and unswerving love. She belongs to him as much as she belongs to Weatherbury.

Bathsheba and the community

Now we are nearing the heart of the matter. Hardy's presentation of Bathsheba enmeshes her in the life of her community and finally identifies her with the qualities of that life, particularly as they are evident in Gabriel Oak.

In marrying Troy she broke away from that life. It is significant that the marriage itself takes place not in Weatherbury, not within the locality, but in a distant city. Bath is not just some way away - it represents a different world. That point is firmly made:

> 'Well, 'tis a curious place, to say the least,' observed Moon; 'and it must be a curious people that live therein.' (chapter 33)

Troy as destroyer

Troy himself (whose very name is that of a city that fell to destruction) consistently disrupts the traditional pattern of farming life. His skills are with the sword, not the plough; he wants to alter the farmhouse; he abuses the barn, makes the farmhands drunk; the profits of farming are wasted in gambling. He is restless and pleasure-seeking, lives only for the moment – attitudes totally athwart the steady cycles of patient labour that the farmer must nurture.

Bathsheba has painfully to learn that there is no way in which the life-styles of Weatherbury and of Troy can be reconciled.

Boldwood isolated

This essential theme is present, but with a different emphasis, in Boldwood. He of course is a farmer; but he is withdrawn and seems to have little integration with local society. (We never, for example, see him playing the role of the local squire as might have been expected.) Perhaps there is even a hint here that without roots drawing vitality from the ground-soil of community life a personality may lack the strength and vigour to survive.

The main point made about Boldwood complements the one made through Troy: he too abandons his responsibilities as a farmer. His neglected ricks are destroyed by the storm just as his own life-style is ravaged by the violence of his love. It is not fitting in this story that a character so damagingly extreme and unbalanced should marry the heroine: she belongs to the faithful shepherd.

Oak the centre

For Gabriel Oak is the still centre of this world. Violence is alien to him. He is never at the mercy of his feelings, but always master of himself. Troy wields a sword; Boldwood fires a gun; Oak's only weapon is the tool of his trade, which he displays at the hiring-fair: a shepherd's crook.

His skills are not only those of his trade. He is generally a man of knowledge and resource: organising the dousing of the rick fires, covering the ricks in the storm; becoming bailiff to Bathsheba and being invited to run Boldwood's farm; playing the flute sweetly and possessor of a library 'from which he had acquired more sound information by diligent perusal than many a man of opportunities had done from a furlong of laden shelves'. And as we have seen in Chapter 2, there are many occasions when his skills and resourcefulness come to Bathsheba's rescue.

A man skilled in his craft, able to direct and organise, possessing a range of gifts and personal qualities, Gabriel is respected by all who know him, from Boldwood to Cainy Ball. He is a man absolutely at one with his situation and environment, devoting his life to the welfare of his sheep, the farm for which he is responsible, his fellow workers and the woman he loves. There is an inner stability and balance to his character: 'for his intellect and his emotions were clearly separated'. In this he is the direct opposite of Boldwood, who is totally thrown off balance. He is a man who, like Hamlet's Horatio, 'is not passion's slave'.

Passion in this story is violently destructive, its energy disrupts. This is not to say that Gabriel lacks strong feelings - far from it; but he always has them under control. Hardy himself was a deeply reticent personality and it may well be that his instinct was to admire men who could contain and harness their inmost selves.

Certainly Oak gives himself not to passion, but to his community. His role is perhaps best defined in the poem from which Hardy took his title, Thomas Gray's *Elegy*. We shall be looking at this poem again later. The verse appropriate to our discussion here runs:

> Far from the madding crowd's ignoble strife,
>   Their sober wishes never learn'd to stray;
> Along the cool sequester'd vale of life
>   They kept the noiseless tenor of their way.

Without ambition outside his own sphere, Oak keeps quietly to his 'vale of life' and allows his 'sober wishes' to guide him in all he does.

Bathsheba and Oak in harmony

So when Bathsheba and Gabriel finally come together it is not in a blaze of passion. Their union has a strength that comes from shared experience, a common commitment to a working life and the sense of good fellowship derived from this.

The final paragraph describing their love is quietly emphatic:

> Theirs was that substantial affection which arises (if any arise at all) when the two who are thrown together begin first by knowing the rougher sides of each other's character, and not the best till further on, the romance growing up in the interstices of a mass of hard prosaic reality . . . the compounded feeling proves itself to be the only love which is strong as death - that love which many waters cannot quench, nor the floods drown, beside which the passion usually called by the name is evanescent as steam. (chapter 56)

Not many readers today will recognise the quotation that Hardy has incorporated here from the Bible, from the Song of Solomon. It is interesting to look at the whole passage.

> Set me as a seal upon your heart, as a seal upon your arm,
> for love is strong as death, jealousy is cruel as the grave.
> Its flashes are flashes of fire, a most vehement flame.
> Many waters cannot quench love, neither can floods
> drown it.
> If a man offered for love all the wealth of his house, it
> would be utterly scorned.
>
> (Song of Solomon, chapter 8: 6, 7)

How apt it all is. 'Flashes of fire' recalls Troy; 'jealousy' and 'all the wealth of his house' Boldwood. The Song of Solomon is a passionate outpouring of which these verses are the culminating statement. The implication is that the love between Bathsheba and Gabriel flows with a vital and powerful current even though it shows none of the flashiness of Troy, a brilliance that dazzles but is not sustained.

Life sustained

In looking at the main characters in the way that we have, a clear statement emerges.

Unless love is a true partnership, a working relationship as well as a meeting of hearts, it is insecure. As far as the people in this story are concerned the needs and patterns of a country society, unchanged in its cycles and rhythms for centuries, give meaning and purpose to existence. To ignore or neglect or disturb these patterns is to destroy the whole balance of relationships, both personal and social.

The job of a soldier is ultimately to take life. Troy indirectly causes Fanny's death, in effect destroys Boldwood, and threatens to destroy the life of the farm. His instinct is to take, not to give. He is illegitimate and his socially divided parentage implies a lack of central focus and balance: he is an outsider.

Gabriel, as we have seen, is wholly an 'insider' – by birth, by occupation and by nature. His role is to sustain life:

> He returned to the hut, bringing in his arms a new-born lamb, consisting of four legs large enough for a full-grown sheep, united by a seemingly inconsiderable membrane about half the substance of the legs collectively, which constituted the animal's entire body just at present.

The little speck of life he placed on a wisp of hay before the small stove, where a can of milk was simmering. (chapter 2)

Even Gabriel's physical movement is expressive of his qualities:

Oak's motions, though they had a quiet energy, were slow and their deliberateness accorded well with his occupation. Fitness being the basis of beauty, nobody could have denied that his steady swings and turns in and about the flock had elements of grace. (chapter 2)

There we have it: 'Fitness being the basis of beauty'. As a trained architect Hardy knew how a building satisfies only when it is 'fit' – when it performs exactly and honestly the purpose for which it is intended. It cannot be a 'beautiful' building if it does not in the first place perform its job purposefully. This idea is given expression in the description of the barn:

Here at least the spirit of the ancient builders was at one with the spirit of the modern beholder. Standing before this abraded pile, the eye regarded its present usage, the mind dwelt upon its past history, with a satisfied sense of functional continuity throughout – a feeling almost of gratitude, and quite of pride, at the permanence of the idea which had heaped it up. (chapter 22)

Integrity of living

Gabriel and the barn are both metaphors for the 'fitness' that Hardy celebrates in this story as an essential quality of life having solidity, integrity and beauty. It survives staunchly – as the oak, as the 'heavy-pointed arches of stone . . . the dusky, filmed, chestnut roof, braced and tied in by huge collars'.

This concept is surely of permanent value and relevance. Modern society is increasingly hectic and mobile. Traditional skills and the communities these fostered – in textiles, in ship-building, in steel-making, in coal-mining – are in the throes of painful adjustment. Many jobs involve more frequent upheaval and change of location than used to be the case. We are told that the working man of the twenty-first century must expect either to change his job frequently or not assume he can justify his life in terms of his work as there will not be enough occupations to satisfy our sense of a traditional working life.

We may be in danger of losing the idea of integrity of work, work rooted in a particular environment and settled culture. However, we are also aware of this danger: the preservation of craftsmanship, the nurture of the vitality of local communities, the search for permanence and steadiness in a world of disorienting mobility – these are all apprehensions that are alive today and to some extent countering the centrifugal tendency of technological advance to tug us away from any firm centre to our lives.

The values centred in Oak are ones we should continue to hold in high regard and not think of as belonging merely to a distant way of life without any meaning or relevance to modern society.

In personal relationships, too, should we not also learn to be cautious of the passionate excess that may dangerously weaken our hold on calmer qualities, less exciting no doubt, but also in the long run more deeply enriching because they link us to proven virtues of honest commitment? One lesson of *Far from the Madding Crowd* is that relationships can destroy as well as create and we do well to think twice before setting out for the 'wilder shores' of love.

3.3 ENVIRONEMENT

The term 'Novels of Character and Environment' was the cue for this discussion of the themes of *Far from the Madding Crowd*. We have thought about 'Character' in this context and must now consider 'Environment'.

Nineteenth-century Dorset

In the mid-nineteenth century Dorset was still a very remote and largely undisturbed county. To Londoners in particular it seems a total backwater inhabited by a kind of rural clown for whom the contemptuous term was 'Hodge'. For Hardy, whose whole background and upbringing was in Dorset, this patronising ignorance was a slanderous misrepresentation. In an article entitled *The Dorsetshire Labourer* he made the point vigorously:

> This supposedly real but highly conventional Hodge is a degraded being of uncouth manner and aspect, stolid understanding, and snail-like movement.

Hardy goes on to suppose that a city gentleman actually comes to stay with a despised 'Hodge':

> Six months pass, and our gentleman leaves the cottage, bidding goodbye with genuine regret. The great change in his perception is that Hodge, the dull, unvarying, joyless one, has ceased to exist for him. He has become disintegrated into a number of dissimilar

fellow-creatures, men of many minds, infinite in difference . . .
Dick the carter, Bob the shepherd, and Sam the ploughman.

Consistently throughout his novels, Hardy was to create distinctively
individual country people whose integrity and honesty are set against
malicious or unfeeling outsiders who have no understanding of the pattern
of living that fosters an agricultural community. Troy in *Far from the
Madding Crowd*, Alec d'Urberville in *Tess of the d'Urbervilles* and, in some
respects, Farfrae in *The Mayor of Casterbridge* are 'foreigners' whose
attitudes are ultimately destructive.

Let us now look more closely at the novel itself to see in what particular
ways it gives us a sense of the wholesomeness and richness of community.

Wessex

The village that Hardy called 'Weatherbury' was not truly an invention -
except in its name. It is essentially the village of Puddletown, which is only
a couple of miles from Higher Bockhampton where Hardy was writing
Far from the Madding Crowd. So he was physically at the centre of the
region he describes in the novel.

Nearly all his novels are localised in the sense that their stories are
set in Dorset and the counties which neighbour it - Devon, Somerset,
Wiltshire, Hampshire. And it is in the opening to chapter 50 of *Far from
the Madding Crowd* that he first gave a name to the whole area - as he
explains in his Preface:

> In reprinting this story for a new edition I am reminded that it
> was in the chapters of 'Far from the Madding Crowd', as they
> appeared month by month in a popular magazine, that I first ven-
> tured to adopt the word 'Wessex' from the pages of early English
> history, and give it a fictitious significance as the existing name of
> the district once included in that extinct kingdom.

Even by the time Hardy was writing the Preface the name he had
resurrected was coming into general use;

> I did not anticipate that this application of the word to modern
> story would extend outside the chapters of these particular chronicles.
> But it was soon taken up elsewhere . . .

And it has stuck. A Tourist Board, for example, has recently issued a
'Leisure Map' of the central southern counties which they entitle 'Wessex'
- presumably assuming that the term is now known to everyone and does
not need explaining.

If it is possible for you, do take an opportunity to go down to Dorset and wander round the setting of *Far from the Madding Crowd*. Although much, of course, has altered since 1874 the pace of change in Dorset still happily lags behind that of counties nearer London. The essential features of the villages and landscape remain close enough to those Hardy himself knew to make an excursion very rewarding. His father's cottage at Higher Bockhampton is in the care of the National Trust and can be visited. It is moving to stand in the very rooms in which *Far from the Madding Crowd* was written, to look at the view Hardy saw while writing.

So Wessex was there and is there; it is vital to our understanding of Hardy to sense its reality. In *Far from the Madding Crowd* the Wessex presented is not so much landscape as a place of work, a community of farming folk. Compared to other Wessex novels – for example, *The Return of the Native* or *The Woodlanders* or *Tess of the d'Urbervilles* – *Far from the Madding Crowd* does not linger on the countryside as such. We have few descriptions of the rural context. In fact, buildings are of much greater significance than pasture or woodlands or heath. Gabriel's shepherd's hut, the malthouse, Bathsheba's farm, the great barn, the Shottsford Corn Exchange, the 'Buck's Head' inn, Boldwood's house – these are the typical settings. The context of the story is created by man, by a working community, rather than by nature. Even the outdoor scenes are associated with farm work: the chalk-pit where Gabriel loses his flock, the fields where he saves the 'blasted' sheep or where the sheep-dipping takes place, the ricks in the farmyard. Only locations in which Troy is placed have no farming associations: the barracks, the hollow in the ferns, Bath, Lulwind Cove, the circus tent. Surely this is deliberate and revealing?

Weatherbury: social structure

It is not only the locations, but also the characters, which are so closely integrated with farming. Everyone (apart from very minor characters such as the doctor or the circus people) is directly involved in the business of farming, particularly of sheep-farming.

The society that Hardy portrays is limited to the world of farming: its apex is represented by a gentleman-farmer, its base by the labourers on Bathsheba's farm. There are virtually no professional or middle-class people. Hardy deliberately concentrated on a community that had a single centre and a unified structure. Everyone belongs. Even Troy has the potential to contribute and at moments shows a willingness to do so – helping in the hayfields and hiving the bees. He is also devoted to a country girl who was employed as a servant on Bathsheba's farm. Finally, everyone is judged by the contribution they make to the community.

As we have seen, the essential criterion is established in Gabriel Oak. It is his skills and commitment that nourish and sustain, his foresight and resolution that forestall disaster. Troy represents exactly the opposite: the negative pole to Gabriel's positive. Bathsheba is distracted from her positive role by her infatuation with Troy. Boldwood abandons his responsibilities as farmer and employer.

Bathsheba as employer

Yet Bathsheba never wholly neglects her responsibilities as Boldwood does. From the start, although everyone is surprised by her boldness in taking over her uncle's farm, she makes a very good job of it:

> Oak walked on to the village, still astonished at the re-encounter with Bathsheba . . . and perplexed at the rapidity with which the unpractised girl of Norcombe had developed into the supervising and cool woman. (chapter 7)

Joseph Poorgrass, on hearing of her inheritance of the farm, shows a working-man's immediate concern: 'And how do she pay?' Well, she pays generously – but not foolishly. Before she pays her work-people she questions them in turn about their responsibilities and skills, asking for reference when she is in doubt:

> 'Are they satisfactory women?' she inquired softly. (chapter 10)

When the answers are to her satisfaction everyone is given 'ten shillings in addition as a small present, as I am a newcomer'. (chapter 10)

She is clearly the boss, dismissing Pennyways peremptorily and even having the nerve to ask Gabriel whether he understands his duties, before rising 'with a pretty dignity' to announce:

> 'Now mind, you have a mistress instead of a master. I don't yet know my powers or my talents in farming; but I shall do my best, and if you serve me well, so shall I serve you. Don't any unfair ones among you (if there are any such, but I hope not) suppose that because I'm a woman I don't understand the difference between bad goings-on and good . . . I shall be up before you are awake; I shall be afield before you are up; and I shall have breakfasted before you are afield.' (chapter 10)

What an excellent employer she is: not afraid to assert her authority where necessary, making clear she will stand for no nonsense, paying fairly in return for honest work, setting a tough example of hard commitment herself. Perhaps the phrase we should particularly note is:

> 'I shall do my best, and if you serve me well, so shall I serve you.'

Here she implies mutual service and respect. Although firmly in control she shows no condescension or patronage towards her employees. This kind of relationship is wholly admirable: there is trust, warmth, efficiency – and a great sense of stability: this is how things should be, we feel. The new mistress is not going to upset that settled pattern of working with which everyone is familar. Joseph Poorgrass's verdict is conclusive: 'A happy time for us.'

Perhaps Hardy may have had at the back of his mind memories of his father, an easy-going, kindly man who, as a small builder, employed a number of hands who were paid at a small window at the back of the Higher Bockhampton cottage.

Interestingly, Bathsheba does not allow either the disturbing attentions of Boldwood or her infatuation with Troy to override her duties and responsibilities as an employer. The contrast with Boldwood in this respect is made explicit at the opening of chapter 19:

> In contemplating Bathsheba as a woman, he had forgotten the accidents of her position as an agriculturalist – that being as much of a farmer, and as extensive a farmer as himself, her probable whereabouts was out-of-doors at this time of the year. This, and the other oversights Boldwood was guilty of, were natural to the mood, and still more natural to the circumstances.

Oversights may be natural to Boldwood – but not to Bathsheba. She supervises the sheep-dipping; whatever it costs her pride she will beg Gabriel's assistance when the life of her sheep are at stake. At the sheep-shearing she is not just a useless spectator:

> Bathsheba, after throwing a glance here, a caution there, and lecturing one of the younger operators who had allowed his last sheep to go off among the flock without re-stamping it with her initials. (chapter 22)

Although – significantly – after Troy has spoken to her in the hay-mead 'Bathsheba could not face the haymaking now . . . she retreated homeward', she does not ever intend to abandon the farm – as her work-people expect her to do:

> 'If he marry her, she'll gie up farming.'

After her marriage she remains concerned for her hands, imploring Troy not to give them strong drink at the harvest-supper:

> 'No, don't give it to them, pray don't, Frank! It will only harm them.' (chapter 36)

Also of course she helps Gabriel cover the ricks in the storm - in striking contrast to Boldwood, as we have already noted. The seriousness of her sense of responsibility is underlined when she hears of Fanny Robin's death: she will not allow Boldwood to send a waggon to fetch the body:

> 'Indeed I shall not let Mr Boldwood do any such thing - I shall do it! Fanny was my uncle's servant, and, although I only knew her for a couple of days, she belongs to me.' (chapter 41)

Only a few days after the traumatic episode over Fanny's corpse she is attending the cornmarket. The farm must be kept going; legal and financial problems must be faced up to, even by those whose heart is breaking:

> She had latterly been in great doubt as to what the legal effects of her marriage would be upon her position; and only one point was clear - that in the event of her own or her husband's inability to meet the agent at the forthcoming January rent-day, very little consideration would be shown, and, for that matter, deserved. Once out of the farm the approach of poverty would be sure. (chapter 48)

As time passes without any news of Troy, Bathsheba does not indulge in listless abandon; there is work to be done and she does it. 'She kept the farm going and raked in her profits', even though with little sense of purpose or achievement. And she also appoints Oak as bailiff. The contrast with Boldwood is sustained:

> Much of his wheat and all his barley of that season had been spoilt by the rain. It sprouted, grew into intricate mats, and was ultimately thrown to the pigs in armfuls. (chapter 49)

It is not cynical to observe that she is in part prompted to open her heart to Gabriel by the thought that if he were to emigrate (as he has told her he might) her farm would suffer:

> She was bewildered too by the prospect of having to rely on her own resources again: it seems to herself that she never could again acquire

energy sufficient to go to market, barter and sell. Since Troy's death Oak had attended all sales and fairs for her, transacting her business at the same time with his own. What should she do now? (chapter 56)

Together at last they do not move into any haze of a sentimental sunset:

> He accompanied her up the hill, explaining to her the details of his forthcoming tenure of the other farm. They spoke very little of their mutual feelings. (chapter 56)

This really does sum it all up, doesn't it? Lovers together, united at last – and what do they talk about? Love? The old times? The happiness to come? No!: 'details of his forthcoming tenure'. Here is indeed the 'mass of hard prosaic reality'. Their love does not need words or gesture; it is founded on 'good-fellowship, camaraderie'. It is 'the only love which is strong as death'.

These two are justly rewarded because they have never betrayed the loyalties of their calling. Whenever the welfare of their environment has been threatened they have both worked to protect the means by which that welfare is sustained: crops are saved, sheep are rescued, wages are paid, tenure secured.

The workfolk

When we leave Bathsheba and Gabriel they are in the only appropriate company, that of their workfolk:

> The rays fell upon a group of male figures gathered upon the gravel in front, who, when they saw the newly-married couple in the porch, set up a loud 'Hurrah!' and at the same moment bang again went the cannon in the background, followed by a hideous clang of music from a drum, tambourine, clarionet, serpent, hautboy, tenor-viol, and double-bass – the only remaining relics of the original Weatherbury band – venerable worm-eaten instruments, which had celebrated in their own persons the victories of Marlborough, under the fingers of the forefathers of those who played them now. (chapter 57)

Their music is made on instruments that have been handed down from generation to generation: the continuity of tradition is needed for that 'note of admiration' sounded by these honest people. Bathsheba and Gabriel and the farmhands are at one in their job: 'Then Oak laughed and Bathsheba smiled.' Joseph gives a 'cheerful sigh' and has the last word: 'Since 'tis as 'tis, why, it might have been worse and I feel my thanks accordingly.'

The part played by the work-people in enriching the sense of a real and life-sustaining environment is vital to the novel and one we must now consider.

We can start by thinking about the title, *Far from the Madding Crowd*. As we saw earlier in the commentary, this is a quotation from an eighteenth-century poem, *Elegy* by Thomas Gray. The poet describes himself sitting in a country churchyard (no doubt little different from the one at Stinsford very close to Hardy's birthplace) and thinking about the lives of the humble country folk buried there. He warns worldly and ambitious people not to despise their simplicity:

> Let not Ambition mock their useful toil,
> Their homely joys, and destiny obscure;
> Nor Grandeur hear with a disdainful smile,
> The short and simple annals of the poor.

He goes on to consider the possible talent that might have been aborted or frustrated by the harshness and poverty of their lives; then he points out that though they may not have achieved anything famous or remarkable, neither have they been guilty of sophisticated corruption. He continues:

> Far from the madding crowd's ignoble strife,
> Their sober wishes never learn'd to stray;
> Along the cool sequester'd vale of life
> They kept the noiseless tenor of their way.

So Hardy in one sense took his cue from a poem which championed the values of humble and honest country existence. These people, said Gray, have a level-headed, decent outlook beside which the more urgent, frantic pace of city life, that of the 'madding crowd' is seen to be fiercely vicious, 'ignoble strife'.

This is of course a partial and, to some extent, sentimentalised view. Not *all* country people lead a sober, rewarding life; not *all* city-dwellers take part in a ruthless rat-race. But both Gray and Hardy are taking sides: their concern is to counter the ignorant and arrogant assumption of 'ambition' and 'grandeur' that all farming people are 'Hodges.' The writers are celebrating the integrity and value of rural society.

However, Hardy's vision was far sharper and more localised than that of Gray. The eighteenth-century poet was no countryman, born and bred among the realities of country life. His is a rather distant, philosophical sympathy; he is concerned to make a general moral point – do not despise humble people. Hardy gives us the physical, social and economic texture of a real community, lived in and intimately understood.

So his work-people are not simply the general class of labourers outlined by Gray, but a distinctively individualised cluster of characters: the maltster, Joseph Poorgrass, Cain Ball, Jan Coggan, Liddy, Fanny Robin and all the others.

Hardy uses this group to several purposes in the novel. They will be discussed here only in the context of the social environment, their other aspects being considered in Chapter 4, 'Technical Features',

It is in the malthouse that we first see them as Gabriel opens the door:

> The room inside was lighted only by the ruddy glow from the kiln mouth, which shone over the floor with the streaming horizontality of the setting sun, and threw upwards the shadows of all facial irregularities in those assembled around. The stone-flag floor was worn into a path from the doorway to the kiln, and into undulations everywhere. (chapter 8)

The place is warm and time-worn. So is the maltster:

> This aged man was now sitting opposite the fire, his frosty white hair and beard overgrowing his gnarled figure like the grey moss and lichen upon a leafless apple-tree. (chapter 8)

Gabriel is immediately made welcome and then identified by the maltster:

> 'That's never Gable Oak's grandson over at Norcombe – never!' he said, as a formula expressive of surprise, which nobody was supposed to take literally.
> 'My father and my grandfather were old men of the name of Gabriel,' said the shepherd placidly.
> 'Thought I knowed the man's face as I seed him on the rick – thought I did!' (chapter 8)

The maltster's son and grandson continue the conversation recalling acquaintances known to them and to Gabriel. Local tradition and custom are cited:

> ''twas only last Purification Day in the very world, when the use-money is gied away to the second-best poor folk, you know, shepherd.'

(This was the annual distribution to needy people of money accumulating as interest on charitable endowments.)

After Gabriel has been invited to drink from the 'God-forgive-me' mug and offered bread and bacon the conversation drifts to local gossip and stories all hugely enjoyed by the company.

What a delight the whole scene is. Fun, of course, with several richly eccentric characters – but not merely clowning. It is the sense of shared life that is so vivid: people are known and noted, oddities enjoyed but accepted. There is no malice, no rivalry. On the contrary, there is courtesy and good fellowship. The dense warmth of the malthouse presided over by the incredibly ancient maltster is a glowing image of a whole quality of life.

In his *Life* Hardy grieved over the passing of this kind of tightly-knit community:

> Village tradition – a vast mass of unwritten folklore, local chronicle, local topography, and nomenclature – is absolutely sinking, has nearly sunk, into eternal oblivion. I cannot recall a single instance of a labourer who still lives on the farm where he was born, and I can only recall a few who have been five years on their present farms. Thus you see, there being no continuity of environment in their lives, there is no continuity of information, the names, stories and relics of one place being speedily forgotten under the incoming facts of the next.

However, the changing conditions of the latter part of the nineteenth century, although they eroded these older traditions and loyalties, did on the whole improve the situation of the agricultural labourer. In *The Dorsetshire Labourer* Hardy noted:

> These quaint and charming traditions probably had to go if the labourers were ever to be freed from their shackles. It is only the old story that progress and picturesqueness do not harmonise. They are losing their individuality, but they are widening the range of their ideas, and gaining in freedom. It is too much to expect them to remain stagnant and old-fashioned for the pleasure of romantic spectators.

This last point is an important one that needs to be considered.

A romantic presentation?

Everyone knows that older people grieve for 'the good old days'. We tend to romanticise the past, remembering with affection the moments of fun and friendship. So, in creating these likeable rustics, simple-minded and warm-hearted, is Hardy guilty of a distortion? Is he being untruthful –

giving us what he would like to believe rather than a wholly honest account? These are not easy questions to answer.

In part the answer must be 'yes'. Hardy has not quite given the full picture, not in this novel. But he was to do so later, very unsparingly. The hardships and humiliations, exploitations and injustices that country folk faced are given unflinchingly and grimly in nearly every novel that he wrote after *Far from the Madding Crowd*.

So we cannot say that he is a superficially romantic novelist who evaded the harsh truth. In fact he was frequently accused of being too harsh and pessimistic. No, Hardy knew well enough the tough nature of life in his Wessex and did not in any way flinch from presenting it – when it was to his purpose to do so.

This was not his purpose here. While his later vision is relentlessly tragic, in *Far from the Madding Crowd* he created a world that absorbs tragedy and recovers confidence in itself. More of this later. At the moment the point to grasp is that the primarily joyous and positive treatment of the chorus of workfolk is in keeping with the essentially buoyant mood of the novel as a whole.

So the emphasis is on comradeship and fun. These people, however simple, are, with few exceptions, good-humoured, tolerant, God-fearing folk with a strong sense of loyalty and duty.

They are also unreliable, incompetent and subservient. They get in a hopeless tangle trying to put out the rick fire; none of them can cope with the 'blasted' sheep; they are all dead drunk during the harvest storm; Joseph Poorgrass is afflicted with the 'multiplying eye' at a critical moment. They share some of the characteristics of the sheep which they tend, showing no initiative or capacity for leadership. They are all economically dependent on Bathsheba, having no means of livelihood beyond their farm wages.

So it is not an entirely favourable or sentimental presentation that is given.

Yet the sense we are left with is surely the one that dominates that last chapter which we have already considered. Allegiance to their masters, expressed in clumsy but spontaneous rejoicing celebrates 'Long life and happiness to neighbour Oak and his comely bride'. All is well in this family of fellow workers: *'neighbour* Oak' – that is the heart of it: he is one of them, they belong to him. There is a strong trust that providence is on their side:

'Hurrah!' said Coggan with a swelling heart. 'God's above the devil yet!' (chapter 55)

We can now include the work-people together with Gabriel and Bathsheba in that idea of 'fitness', of belonging rightfully that was discussed earlier. So Hardy's theme of community we see to be threaded right through the fabric of the novel, drawing together heroine-farmer, shepherd-hero and the people whom they both serve and employ.

3.4 'PASTORAL'

Fully to understand Hardy's themes in *Far from the Madding Crowd* we need to consider two other aspects of his writing. They touch on 'character' and 'environment', but are distinct.

The literary tradition

The first is the 'pastoral' convention. This term is used to describe a kind of writing virtually as old as literature itself since it can be found in Greek and Roman authors. 'Pastoral' is the adjective from 'pastor' which means a herdsman or shepherd. So in the first place, 'pastoral' means simply 'having to do with a shepherd'; but we have to look further.

People have always cherished a dream or vision of some kind of ideally happy life where there are no horrors or pain or tragedies; writers have given expression to this dream in all sorts of ways, creating imaginary worlds where the pressures of real life have no place, all evil and harm are banished and lovers wander, happy and secure.

One version of this kind of never-never-land is an idealised world of the shepherd. Here there are no threats, no challenges – beyond the occasional wolf to be chased away. The shepherd guards his flock in an endlessly sunny countryside; his only diversion is his love for a sweet country girl. Such a fiction is very slight and fragile, and of course it has hardly anything to do with the lonely and demanding life of a real working shepherd.

Yet it has remained imaginatively very powerful, undergoing all sorts of development and variation in the history of European literature, but persisting in answer to our perpetual craving for the possibility of an existence from which 'the heavy and the weary weight of all this unintelligible world' is lifted.

Far from the Madding Crowd is in some respects a variation on this theme. The loyal shepherd woos his girl, sees her taken away by a 'wolf', but gets her in the end. There is no equivalent to Boldwood in this version. Interestingly he in fact wasn't there when Hardy first gave an indication of the story to Leslie Stephen, the editor of the *Cornhill Magazine* in which *Far from the Madding Crowd* was first published. Stephen had been impressed by an earlier novel of Hardy's and had written to say that he would be happy to publish Hardy's next work. In reply Hardy said that his story would be 'a pastoral tale with a pastoral title', adding that the chief characters would probably be a young woman-farmer, a shepherd and a sergeant of cavalry.

Various suggestions have been made to account for Boldwood's absence in this early summary and the important role he was finally given. These will be considered elsewhere.

Ballad tradition

Yet one could say that, although not really appropriate to the pastoral tradition, Boldwood does perhaps belong to another powerful form of story which also lies behind *Far from the Madding Crowd*: that of the ballad.

Ballads are stories in verse, often anonymous, describing in simple form dramatic encounters of one kind or another. Ballads are mentioned by Hardy as being a part of that cultural tradition that he saw slipping away during his own lifetime. He certainly heard many in his childhood and indeed he wrote several himself. They are part of his imaginative awareness.

Very often ballads tell of violent love and of tragedies. The relationships of the main characters in *Far from the Madding Crowd* are certainly the kind of situation out of which ballads are made. It would not be difficult to take the essentials of the story and retell them in ballad form.

The influence of the pastoral and the ballad traditions combine to give a particular flavour to *Far from the Madding Crowd*. Both very simple forms, they are of course subdued into the much more complex structure of the novel so as to be hardly discernible. For example, the realities of farming life, its difficulties and stresses are a vital element, whereas they have no place in the simpler forms of pastoral and ballad.

Yet the fact that the story is finally a happy one, that the faithful shepherd wins his love; the ways in which the story moves forward in harmony with the rhythms of the sheep-farming year; the sense of an integrated and healthy community – all these aspects have their ultimate source in the pastoral mode of writing.

It is a mode that is displaced in the most important of Hardy's later novels. The sense that environment and character are at one, that a tradition of living has a strength in its continuity and familiarity – this gives way to a troubled vision where dislocation thrusts people's lives out of their known and trusted paths, love turns sour and fulfilment is thwarted.

There is no space in this commentary to follow through Hardy's development. It must be enough to indicate that a comment such as Coggan's 'Hurrah! God's above the devil yet' would be deeply inappropriate in the later novels. Gabriel Oak's traditional skills are replaced by Clym Yeobright's ineffective innovations (*The Return of the Native*); Henchard, Gabriel's equivalent as a country craftsman, finds himself isolated and passed over (*The Mayor of Casterbridge*); the country-girl's love is blighted by seduction (*Tess of the d'Urbervilles*).

So *Far from the Madding Crowd* can be seen, if we look back over the whole perspective of Hardy's writing, as a sort of farewell tribute, an affectionate goodbye to an inheritance. The act of writing was in itself a return of the native: Hardy had come back from London to his origin, his roots. Two of his previous novels (*Under the Greenwood Tree* and *A Pair of Blue Eyes*) were beginning to receive favourable reviews; an influential publisher wanted his work. He was confident, absorbed. The opening chapters in particular of *Far from the Madding Crowd* are alive with a buoyancy and vitality that may well reflect this mood, and even though the suicide of his close friend, Horace Moule, happened while he was in the middle of writing and very probably contributed to the deepening sense of tragedy in the central part of the novel, it did not prevent the story shaping towards a fulfilled, serene conclusion.

It is certainly significant that the great storm does no lasting damage. Not only are the ricks saved; Gabriel and Bathsheba are brought closer together during it. Although disaster comes to Troy, Boldwood and Fanny, the central pair survive both natural disasters and chance accidents. People are not all overwhelmed either by natural forces or by misfortune.

In this respect again, *Far from the Madding Crowd* differs from the later novels where consistently Hardy places his characters at the mercy of a vindictive universe and ironic twists of fate.

3.5 'DESTINY OBSCURE'?

Man as a victim of a cruelly indifferent universe is an idea closely associated with Hardy. We need to think about it briefly just because it has hardly any place in *Far from the Madding Crowd*. We glimpse it possibly when the ugly gargoyles spew out rainwater in seeming contempt on the flowers Troy places on Fanny's grave. However, this incident is certainly not typical of events in the novel. It is more in keeping with the view of life given in *Tess of the d'Urbervilles*.

When Tess, with her younger brother, looks up at the stars they are seen as

> cold pulses . . . beating amid the black hollows above, in serene dissociation from those two wisps of human life.

Her brother asks her how far away they are and whether God is on the other side of them. Then he asks:

> 'Did you say the stars were worlds, Tess?'
> 'Yes.'
> 'All like ours?'
> 'I don't know; but I think so. They sometimes seem to be like apples on our stubbard-tree. Most of them splendid and sound - a few blighted.'
> 'Which do we live on - a splendid one or a blighted one?'
> 'A blighted one.'
> ''Tis very unlucky that we didn't pitch on a sound one, when there were so many more of 'em!'
> 'Yes.'

How different a world this is, blighted and surveyed by 'cold pulses', from that of *Far from the Madding Crowd*. In the first place no one concerns himself very much with that ultimate dimension of life which the stars reflect - the place of man in the universe. Most people have their eyes firmly fixed on the ground attending to sheep or to harvest. However, Gabriel does at one point very early in the story look up:

> The sky was clear - remarkably clear - and the twinkling of all the stars seemed to be but throbs of one body, timed by a common pulse. (chapter 2)

Almost every word here gives us an utterly different association from that of the stars that look down on Tess. There they were cold, in black hollows; here they are twinkling in a remarkably clear sky. For Tess the stars were distantly hostile; here they are 'throbs of one body . . . a common pulse'. The sense of oneness, of purposeful community that we have seen to be a central theme of the novel is here given a superbly eloquent image.

What is more, the whole experience of looking up at the stars is described in *Far from the Madding Crowd* as exhilarating:

> To persons standing alone on a hill during a clear midnight such as this, the roll of the world eastward is almost a palpable movement. The sensation may be caused by the panoramic glide of the stars past earthly objects which is perceptible in a few minutes of stillness, or by the better outlook upon space that a hill affords, or by the wind, or by the solitude; but whatever be its origin the impression of riding along is vivid and abiding. (chapter 2)

Our final impression of the novel is also vivid and abiding: its themes are vigorous and life-enhancing. The first thing we meet is Gabriel's smile, Bathsheba's the last. In between there have been storms and tears. But the stars are not hostile, the storm blows itself out, scars heal and a sense of gratitude gives warmth to Joseph's final words: 'I feel my thanks'.

---

4 TECHNICAL FEATURES

4.1 PLOT AND STRUCTURE

A novel is a lengthy and complex construction. It has to be firmly built and held together. It also has to hold the reader's attention. Probably the most effective way to construct the work and make sure the reader doesn't get bored is to tell a good story. This may seem terribly obvious. Yet not all novelists set out to hold our interest by an energetic story-line: they may be more concerned just with people and their relationships; or they may be primarily interested in ideas, in philosophical or religious notions and using the novel as a vehicle for these. They may even despise the story as being something rather crude and limited, all right for a thriller or detective novel but not worth serious attention in its own right.

Hardy of course was not like this. He was a story-teller. Country places are always alive with stories, whether of actual local events or old tales, traditional ballads. Hardy was brought up with these; they were the natural expression of the lives and background of Dorset people.

Striking incidents

The story which is particularly vivid and memorable usually relates some kind of striking, dramatic or odd circumstance. This to Hardy was essential. While some nineteenth-century writers were interested above all in the ordinary conditions of life, believing that the novel ought to explore what is common and usual and part of people's experience Hardy felt that a writer should not concentrate on the humdrum realities of living, but should excite and stimulate the reader with unusual, gripping incidents. He said:

> The recent school of novel writers forget in their insistence on life, and nothing but life, in a plain slice, that a story must be worth the

telling, that a good deal of life is not worth any such thing, and that they must not occupy a reader's time with what he can get at first hand anywhere around him.

A story must be exceptional enough to justify its telling. We tale-tellers are all Ancient Mariners and none of us is warranted in stopping Wedding Guests (in other words, the hurrying public) unless he has something more unusual to relate than the ordinary experience of every average man and woman.

Well, that is Hardy's view and he certainly was true to his own conviction in his writing. How far he is right is another matter. Of course we are intrigued by violent, strange happenings – whether in life or in fiction. But in fiction we must believe in them, at any rate in novels which are out to persuade us of the reality of their fiction. If events become too weird or incredible then the whole structure of the novel will collapse because we won't be able to accept the reality of the people or of what happens to them.

Yet we can also be interested in very ordinary, everyday events and characters: look at the way 'Coronation Street' stays top of the television ratings. So Hardy may have been prejudiced in declaring so roundly that 'the ordinary experience of every average man and woman' was just not worth a story-teller's time. Writing does not all have to be of one kind.

However, we need to think how Hardy's comments relate to *Far from the Madding Crowd*. Is he giving us here 'exceptional' happenings and disregarding 'ordinary experience'?

Clearly there are a number of dramatic episodes, that kind of unforeseen event which either deeply affects people's lives or calls on staunch qualities of character: the loss of Gabriel's sheep, the fire in the ricks, the deaths of Fanny and of Troy.

There is also another type of episode, not necessarily violent or unexpected, but having a very vivid, emphatic stamp: Gabriel meeting Fanny at night, Troy catching Bathsheba's dress in his spur (again at night); the brilliance of his sword-play; Fanny dragging herself along the road; the rain-water from the gargoyles washing away Troy's flowers; the 'Dick Turpin' performance. While none of these scenes is necessarily improbable, or puts any undue strain on our acceptance of their reality, each certainly strikes our imagination sharply. This is very characteristic of Hardy's art. Another quotation from his own thinking helps to define his distinctive idiom:

Art is a changing of the actual proportions and order of things, so as to bring out more forcibly than might otherwise be done that

feature in them which appeals most strongly to the idiosyncrasy of
the artist.

The key phrase here is 'bring out more forcibly'. Hardy is saying that
the story-teller deliberately distorts, gives a stronger emphasis to dramatic
moments than is found in life itself.

However, we have already seen in the previous chapter that there are
two further emphases in *Far from the Madding Crowd* both of which have
the effect of containing or sobering that 'changing of the actual proportion
and order of things' of which Hardy spoke. The first is the realities of
working, farming life, the unremarkable and undramatic matters of tending
sheep, managing a farm, paying employees. The second is the detailed
precision of observation shown throughout the novel which complements
the first reality by a firm sense of people and location convincingly presented.

So a balance is achieved: the story works to seize our imagination with
a series of dramatic or powerful or emphatic scenes deliberately conceived
as a 'changing of the actual proportions and order' of life, both a tele-
scoping and an accelerating technique. Yet the descriptive detail and the
more placid, rhythmic patterns of the farming year give a convincing sense
of those 'actual proportions'.

Finally, however, one must agree that Hardy's stories *are* crowded with
exciting, at times flamboyant, incident. This is one thing we delight in;
he is rightly famous for his 'set' scenes. They are both a strength and a
limitation in his writing. We don't really go to Hardy in the first place
to enter a world that seems our own. His novels have a colouring and a
drama that create worlds of their own.

In establishing that Hardy makes frequent use of strong incident and
encounters we have not yet really even begun to think about the construction of his story, about how the episodes are arranged and related.
This we must now do.

Pressure from the past

As a story the novel is firmly and vigorously constructed. It has the character of a ballad tale, full of romance and challenge, drama and tragedy,
true love finally rewarded. There is also a very firm moral position: the
'villain' is disposed of, the unbalanced lover removed from the scene, the
faithful 'goody' given his just reward.

The pivot on which the story turns is Fanny Robin. She also belongs to
the ballad tradition: a kind of ghost from the past returning to haunt a
central character. Hardy had a fondness for this device. For example,
in *The Mayor of Casterbridge*, Henchard, at the beginning of the story,

sells his wife; many years later the consequences of this action are to destroy him. Again, early in *Tess of the d'Urbervilles*, Tess is seduced and has an illegitimate child; her later confession of this seduction destroys her marriage, condemns her to lonely and harsh suffering.

It is an essentially simple but also very effective narrative device. It is used with a particular twist in *Far from the Madding Crowd*. In *The Mayor of Casterbridge* and *Tess of the d'Urbervilles* the reader has been shown the early events which are later to catch up with the central character and trigger disaster. But in *Far from the Madding Crowd* we have no knowledge whatever that Fanny has been made pregnant by Troy. The fact is entirely concealed until we read the inscription chalked on the coffin: 'Fanny Robin and child'. So we have the drama of a startling revelation, a kind of narrative jolt.

This is in keeping with the whole character of the story that thrusts forward with particular vigour and impetus. There has already been another instance of concealment: the reader knows nothing of Bathsheba's marriage to Troy until Boldwood reads the newspaper cutting that the sergeant flings at him. And time and again we are startled by moments of crisis that rear up unexpectedly: the loss of Gabriel's sheep; the fire in the ricks; the shooting of Troy. Nothing prepares us for these. It is not a technique of suspense - a slow build-up with the reader teased by a half-knowledge of what is going on, intrigued by the mystery, eager to understand fully what is happening. It is rather a kind of assault on the reader, a succession of swift punches from nowhere that catch us off our guard.

Serial form

One incentive to writing in a series of dramatic episodes was provided by the serial form of publication of *Far from the Madding Crowd*. The *Cornhill Magazine* published the story in twelve instalments.

Readers of a serial expect each instalment to keep them interested: if nothing very much happens in the way of excitement or revelations it is only too likely that the reader won't buy the next number of the magazine - and the publisher will not therefore be very pleased with the author. As Hardy believed anyway that a story should be 'exceptional enough to justify its telling' he found little difficulty in meeting the demands of serial writing.

It is interesting to check out the original instalments and see how each contained at least one dramatic or emphatic incident. For example, the first instalment covered chapters 1-5; here we have the loss of Gabriel's sheep. In the second instalment, chapters 6-8, there is the fire in Bathsheba's ricks. In the third, chapters 9-14, Fanny outside the barracks at night. And so on.

It is also important in this form of publication that the end of each instalment should arouse expectations, leave the reader eager to read on. While it is not true that every instalment of *Far from the Madding Crowd* ends on an obviously dramatic note, each is contrived in some way to whet the appetite. The first instalment leaves us with Gabriel destitute, 'a free man with the clothes he stood up in, and nothing more'. So the reader wonders what he will do now, how he will cope with his sudden change of fortune. The second instalment ends with two intriguing pieces of information: Pennyways has been caught stealing; Fanny is missing. The third leaves us wondering what Boldwood will do next: 'To Boldwood it was no longer merely a letter to another man. It was an opportunity.' That a significant change of relationships is under way is deftly indicated by the last sentence in the fifth instalment: 'It was a fatal omission of Boldwood's that he had never once told her she was beautiful.' In the chapter summaries we have already noted that the end of the ninth instalment (chapter 42) gives us a really dramatic moment when we learn of Fanny's child.

So the requirements of serial publication are confidently met throughout the novel. Far from being a limitation or an encumbrance, they help sustain the impetus of the story. There is no danger of it drooping limply or stagnating when the expectations of magazine readers had to be answered.

Shifts in tone

However, the shape and build-up of the novel is not really *dictated* by this form of publication. We can look at *Far from the Madding Crowd* in another way to discern a structure more subtle than a mere succession of well-spaced, lively incidents. For Hardy did not only arrange for an interplay of events; he also manipulated important shifts in the tone and rhythms of this story.

Seen in this way, the first phase of the story covers the first four chapters: they are set, as it were, in a minor key: the phrasing is light, the tone that of pastoral romance – the shepherd woos his sweetheart.

The first presentation of Bathsheba is at the heart of this phase: we spy on her as she betrays an amusing touch of vanity. Observing people in this way while they unconsciously reveal themselves is a device of comedy.

Next we are shown the shepherd busy with the skilful care of his newborn lambs. Outside the night sky has the crisp clarity of winter against which is set the 'sovereign brilliancy' of the star Sirius. Inside, the shepherd's hut is 'cosy and alluring', the firelight sheds a 'genial colour'. And what do we hear? Gabriel's flute.

All these details blend to create a softly lyrical mood, quiet, glowing, restful. The first of many night scenes, this one has a very distinctive tone; it is very different from the bleakness or tension or violence that are going to be part of all the later night scenes.

At daybreak we have the first of those slightly odd, offbeat sort of moments of which Hardy was so fond. Gabriel again watches Bathsheba as she drops backwards over the pony's back with her feet against its shoulders to avoid some overhanging branches. Like Gabriel we are 'amused, perhaps a little astonished'; it's all still warm and light-hearted.

This first phase ends with Gabriel's rather clumsy wooing and Bathsheba's skittish evasions. Nothing that has happened has given any sense whatever of tension or menace. It is a prologue with its own delightful character, but deceptive because it gives hardly any sense of future developments.

The next phase is longer, taking up chapters 5-17. It starts with the sudden changes of fortune we noted in the chapter summaries: Oak goes down, Bathsheba up. Gabriel's disaster is interestingly treated. His reaction isn't one of despair at all; he takes it very staunchly, rather as 'one of those things' and immediately sets about shaping a new life without resentment or brooding or self-pity. (If you happen to know *Tess of the d'Urbervilles* compare Oak's loss with the death of Tess's horse: that *is* taken as a terrible blow.)

This second phase then describes Gabriel finding employment with Bathsheba, gossip at the maltster's, Bathsheba's successful running of the farm and the sending of the valentine. Still no tensions or real drama in all this. However, a contrasting note is being sounded, sombre and ominous. In chapter 7 we hear 'a throb of tragic intensity' and are made aware of 'the penumbra of a very deep sadness' (both when Gabriel comes across Fanny near the churchyard on a cold night). So a shadow is beginning to fall across an otherwise unclouded situation. This encounter, together with Fanny's visit in the snow to Troy's barracks and the misunderstanding that prevents her marriage, menaces the comedy of the malthouse scene and the zest of Bathsheba's farm management.

So in these chapters we have both a relaxed, confident mood, and also a darker one that is at this stage kept distinct, but nevertheless introduces a threatening motif to the orchestration of the story. How skilfully Hardy has manipulated these adjustments!

The third phase takes up chapters 18-23. Boldwood is here brought into the foreground and brings a relentless pressure to bear on Bathsheba. The valentine is no longer a little joke that has misfired; it has triggered a strength of passion that keenly distresses Bathsheba. Nevertheless we are not yet made to feel that we are on the brink of tragedy: the situation is essentially seen as a source of deep embarassment and regret – not exactly comedy, to be sure, but still not violent or tragic. (Notice that Fanny, who is always associated with a tragic mood, does not appear in this phase.) Again, the adjustment is subtle and effective: Boldwood's wooing is very different in character from that of Gabriel in the opening phase, but it is not yet bitter or obsessive.

The fourth phase, from chapter 24 to chapter 35, brings Bathsheba and Troy together and sees them married. It's a fast-moving sequence – very appropriate with the dashing sergeant setting the pace. The concealment from the reader of Bathsheba's marriage is effective in tautening the narrative at this point. Notice that Gabriel and Boldwood are still very much kept in view, the phase ending with the latter's 'terrible sorrow'. The whole sequence brings us to the centre-point of the novel with the main characters locked into an apparently irreversible situation.

The story has now to be precipitated towards its climax. This is to happen in two surges.

The first, from chapter 36 to chapter 47, opens ominously: 'The night had a sinister aspect . . . The moon . . . a lurid metallic look.' The great storm presages tragedy and dominates the first half of this movement of the story. Then Fanny is reintroduced and her tragedy brought to its culmination with Troy leaving the area – it seems for good. We have a succession of oppressively tense night scenes and dramatic encounters which bring the main characters into more intimate and searching contact. All the key scenes are created with great intensity and dramatic bravura. The settings – whether in the lightning on the ricks, on the road to Casterbridge with Fanny, beside her coffin, or in the evil hollow to which Bathsheba flees, or in the churchyard while the gargoyles spout – all vibrate with a strenuously poetic imaginative force that is peculiar to Hardy.

Then we have a brief lull in chapters 48 and 49 – and also a movement forward in time; a kind of subdued bridge passage that leads into the second surge.

This occupies chapters 50-54. Hardy had to construct a sequence at least as dramatic as that of the first surge, but without repeating its devices. He creates the colourful and energetic scene in the circus tent. It could be felt that his invention is straining here. While it is quite possible that Troy should have returned from America to England, joined a circus troupe and found himself finally in Weatherbury giving a performance witnessed by Bathsheba, likelihood is pushed to its limits by the further sudden reintroduction of Pennyways and the incident with the incriminating note that Troy snatches back by making a slit in the tent.

The climactic scene of the shooting is confident and its high drama plausible. The striking behaviour of Bathsheba in laying out the corpse makes a powerful final statement to this sequence, giving her a tragic dignity that emphasises how far she has developed strength of character from the time when we first saw her.

Punctuating the drama and passionate tensions of both these 'surges' that we have followed through there are a number of scenes in which the 'rustics' play a part. We will consider their role in a moment. It is a vital aspect of the rhythmic patterning of the novel.

Meanwhile we are left with a 'coda' in the last chapters, 55–57. There is another time drift and a quiet consummation. Storms and violence and passion have exhausted themselves. We are left with a sense of a cycle completed, a reintegration, a rightful fitness of people and of place.

Role of the workfolk

The workfolk are not used to initiate events or to have any significant bearing on the course of the story with the exception of Joseph Poorgrass's lingering at 'The Buck's Head', which is to have such a dramatic outcome.

Their role in the narrative is to provide a kind of steady ground-bass, a counterpoint to the strident or dark keys in which the principal events are pitched. There is always a warm comedy associated with them, whether they are in the malthouse, in the fields, in the barn, the inn or wherever. Their appearances are carefully timed throughout the story: we never go far without coming across them.

In this way they contribute importantly to the general structure and tone of the novel. Where the lives of the main characters are being wrenched and distorted, this group is undisturbed and essentially unchanged, a centre of balance. (More will be said about the kind of folk they are in Section 4.3.)

Locality

Intimately linked with the farmhands is the locality. The general significance of Wessex in Hardy's work has already been discussed. Here we shall think briefly about its function in the structure of the novel.

Like most of Hardy's novels, *Far from the Madding Crowd* is set in a precise and confined location; in this case, Weatherbury. We have a 'prologue' situated a few miles away (Norcombe hill); Bathsheba goes to Bath (but we don't follow her there); we see Troy and Fanny briefly at the barracks and in Casterbridge, Troy at Lulwind Cove. These excursions apart, the story essentially takes place on the farms of Bathsheba and Boldwood.

The use of a tightly restricted location has the effect of steadying the story, giving it a firm centre. Where there may be a tendency in the main characters to move away (Bathsheba to Bath, Troy to America, Gabriel thinking of emigrating) there is always a strong pull back to the known familar environment. As we virtually stay in one place the story is kept essentially simple: there are no confusing switches between locations. Most of Hardy's novels tend to follow this pattern. The whole narrative development is controlled in many ways by the cycle of the sheep-farming year and the descriptive accounts of the Weatherbury environs, especially, as we have seen, its buildings. We are made aware of a settled, traditional context.

In many of his other novels Hardy creates a physical context that is not reassuring, that seems hostile or indifferent to the welfare of the people within it; but Weatherbury is a place of orderly and profitable work (provided due care and attention is given). It is not forbidding or unfriendly. The great barn is its centre, with its calm, abiding strength; the malthouse with its welcoming warmth and social intimacy is the focus of the farmhands' leisure.

It is not therefore a natural setting for tragedy. Disruption and violence seem against its grain. It is the loyal patience of Oak that is found consistent with its character and the story that fittingly belongs here is one where people who work in harmony with that character are duly rewarded.

Chance and coincidence

No account of a Hardy novel can be complete without a consideration of his use of chance events and coincidence.

In any novel, more unusual or arresting situations are likely to be set up than happen to the average person in everyday existence. This is especially true of Hardy, who, as we have seen, felt that a story should deal in striking incidents.

How to bring these about? – that is the challenge. Well, how do things happen in life? First, we are affected by our own personality and situation; second, by chance events. We have some control over the former, none over the latter. If, for example, we decide to take a job or marry or get our own back on someone, then we have made a conscious decision and we are largely responsible for the consequences. But a tree may fall on us, a vital letter may be lost in the post, a war may break out. Here we are not responsible: they are matters of pure chance.

If a story-teller makes too frequent use of the second kind of happening – the chance event – then the reader may become uneasy, particularly when a great deal is made to depend on a chance event or a coincidence. This is because we like to sense a just pattern of cause and effect in fiction. In life itself a delightful young girl may be badly crippled in a car accident in a senseless and unjust way. We have to accept this. But in a story we want to be reassured that there is a purpose and justice in the human condition; that good people are properly rewarded and bad people punished. We like to feel there is a pattern, a proper control, not just an unrelated series of arbitrary and uncontrollable chance happenings.

In Hardy's later novels tragedy comes to his characters partly through a succession of random and unlikely events. In his short stories also he seemed to subject his characters to a pressure of sudden misfortunes: whatever they do, however hard they try to make sense of their lives, these people are battered by a malicious destiny. The story of Michael Henchard in *The Mayor of Casterbridge* is a good example of this kind of treatment. The cumulative effect is to give us a sense that human beings are victims: life metes out a series of savage and unjust blows that never give them a chance to determine their own lives.

What then do we have in *Far from the Madding Crowd?*

In fact, very little in the way of utterly chance happenings that are nothing to do with the character or situation of the people involved. Really, the loss of Gabriel's sheep and Fanny mistaking the church are the only clear instances. One might perhaps add Bathsheba's inheritance of the farm and the lucky chance that a passing fishing-boat picks up Troy – but neither of these is particularly improbable or overstrained.

There are of course chance happenings in abundance, but these are nearly all either not of great significance (such as Bathsheba's ricks being on fire, Cain Ball spotting Bathsheba in Bath, Troy's bulbs being washed out of Fanny's grave) or are also in part a result of a character's own decisions (sending the valentine, Joseph stopping off for a drink). The only significant coincidence is Bathsheba meeting Troy just when she is about to pledge herself to Boldwood.

Although one often reads of Hardy's abuse of chance and coincidence in constructing his stories, while this may be true of other novels the criticism is really not valid as far as *Far from the Madding Crowd* is concerned.

The chains of cause and effect in the novel are not fashioned out of improbable or malicious freaks of fortune, but out of the characters and their situation. Gabriel falls in love in a very understandable way and remains loyal because he is the sort of man to do so. Bathsheba is preoccupied with her inheritance and does not love Gabriel when she first meets him so she keeps her distance. Fanny's tragedy is that she allowed herself to become pregnant by Troy – not that she mistook the church. Boldwood's passion stems from his repressed nature and not from the valentine (which would have had little enough effect on another type of man). Bathsheba does not marry Troy because he happened to get her dress in a tangle. Nothing untoward causes Troy's behaviour on the farm: he is true to his own nature. It is Joseph's own fault that he gets drunk. And so on.

No, it is not gross coincidence or trivially chance events that shape this story. The situations grow and develop out of character and relationships. That Hardy chose to give us violent and dramatic consequences is in the nature of his art. But these are firmly held in place and out of them is constructed a story that is neither wildly improbable nor an expression of a vindictive power of fate such as hovers over the later novels. Here people essentially determine their own destinies and arrive at a satisfyingly appropriate conclusion. That sense of 'fitness' that we have mentioned already in other contexts is again apparent here. It is an essential aspect of *Far from the Madding Crowd* and one reason why the novel has been so much admired.

4.2 THE PATTERN OF CHARACTERISATION

Restrictions

Love. This is the centre of Hardy's characters in *Far from the Madding Crowd*. Not ideas of ambition; not worldliness or politics or power; not evil or corruption. His people are creatures of passion: their love may smoulder or flare up, be selfish or generous; it may sustain them or destroy them - but it is the heart of their being. If we consider the quality of love shown in each of the main characters we are looking at their centre. Their other characteristics are essentially complementary to their kind of loving.

Bathsheba is at the centre of the novel, as she is the centre of three men's attentions. She knows two kinds of love: one passionate and sexual that answers to only part of her nature; the other quieter and fed not by passion, but by comradeship in shared commitment. Gabriel's love is not that of passion at all. It never throws him off balance, but has a steady centre weighted by that 'deliberateness' which 'accorded well with his occupation'. Troy loves himself, but his character is made more interesting by the unexpected loyalty he shows to Fanny. Boldwood is obsessed, totally thrown off centre. Fanny, although a vital fulcrum in the story, we see little of and know only that she loves Frank Troy with utter commitment.

Apart from some very minor characters who make the briefest of appearances the only other people in the story are the workfolk. We don't see them in love, but they do talk about love and marriage and they do closely follow their mistress's love affairs. As a group they have an important role and some are distinguished individually, but none is the object of any close attention.

This arrangement of characters - four principals enmeshed in a single relationship, Fanny presented only as a function of the story, the rustics as onlookers - is revealing. It is probably safe to say that most other novelists introduce secondary characters who contribute significantly to the story, but not as lovers. They may, for example, belong to the family of a main character, or be part of their professional lives, or neighbours, or rivals in business or in some kind of power struggle.

However, Hardy in *Far from the Madding Crowd* uses none of these types. We are again reminded of the simplicity and confinement of the range of this story which offers a ballad-like tale with an echo of pastoral: lovers seen in the context of a working community. That is what we have. The concentration, the directness that results are both a strength and a limitation.

A contemporary novelist, Henry James, who wrote about sophisticated and wealthy people with great subtlety of insight, was crudely unsympathetic to Hardy's achievement in *Far from the Madding Crowd*. 'The only things we believe in are the sheep and the dogs', he sneered. It could be said that this jibe tells us more about James than it does about Hardy, but it does serve to illustrate the view that Hardy's characters lack range or variety or subtlety.

Certainly Hardy was preoccupied with certain types of personality. The woman of independent spirit who needs time and painful experience to discover what she really wants; the loyal, quiet countryman who bides his time; the dashing, irresponsible outsider – all these appear in other novels than *Far from the Madding Crowd*. They are variations on a theme, reworkings rather than a stock type reproduced mechanically in one novel after another.

They are created with a forceful vitality which ensures that they are not simply two-dimensional or unconvincing. They are also intimately involved with the world in which they live – not detached figures set against a back-drop.

We should now look at the characters individually to try to see their features more clearly and form some judgement about their effectiveness.

Bathsheba

While the men are all constant to basic traits in their character, Bathsheba is to change in a number of ways.

At first she is her own mistress. She looks in the mirror on top of the farm-waggon, likes what she sees and pictures herself dominating a host of admirers. Self-assured and attractive, she enjoys flirting with Gabriel, then rejects him with cool assurance:

> 'I am better educated than you – and I don't love you a bit. That's my side of the case . . . so 'twould be ridiculous.' (chapter 4)

Her poise is not much disturbed by suddenly meeting him again when she is mistress of a farm and he a mere shepherd:

She scarcely knew whether most to be amused at the singularity of the meeting, or to be concerned at its awkwardness . . . Embarrassed she was not. (chapter 7)

We have already discussed the very capable way in which she manages the farm and her workfolk. They have their view of her – and usually they are shrewd enough in their assessments of people. Billy Smallbury has summed her up swiftly: 'She's a very vain feymell'. That his comment is just is confirmed by her irritation at being ignored by Boldwood at the corn market. Hence Liddy's suggestion of sending the valentine to the 'stupid old Boldwood' appeals to her wounded vanity.

Once the valentine is sent she is immediately aware of its result: when Boldwood approaches her at the sheep-shearing she is conscious that 'love was encircling her like a perfume'. His offer of marriage touches her and no doubt pleases her vanity but she does not love him and although in standing and in character he would be a good catch, she is not interested in marriage – her new role as mistress of a farm is too attractive.

She nevertheless continues to feel guilty at having provoked Boldwood's love, her conscience making her flare up at Gabriel when he tells her she is to blame for flirting. So she brings herself to make a half-promise to Boldwood and it seems likely that had she not then met Troy she would have become Mrs Boldwood – but the soldier appeals to her vanity and displaces the farmer:

> It was a fatal omission of Boldwood's that he had never once told her she was beautiful. (chapter 24)

Moreover Troy is handsome. Flattering and masterful, the romantically illegitimate son of an earl – what more could a girl want in a lover? At their next meeting she is all his:

> Her heart erratically flitting hither and thither from excitement, hot, and almost tearful. (chapter 26)

Parallel to her own agony of love runs that of Boldwood. When he passionately rebukes her for accepting Troy, she is devastated:

> Such astounding wells of fevered feeling in a still man like Mr Boldwood were incomprehensible, dreadful. (chapter 31)

Under the dual pressure of her distracted love for Troy and Boldwood's fury of passion, it is not surprising that she makes an ill-considered dash for Bath. Later she tells Gabriel that she went to Bath intending to break off her engagement to Troy. We never know whether she was deluding herself in saying this. However, Troy threatens to desert her for another woman. She is not prepared to become his mistress nor can she bear to lose him. So they are married. She does not see this as blackmail, protesting, 'He was not to blame' and adding the astonishing justification: 'for it was perfectly true about - about his seeing somebody else'. Surely any woman less infatuated than Bathsheba would have felt humiliated and outraged by Troy's behaviour. But she is prepared to accept humiliation and a period of deep suffering begins. An important paragraph in the middle of chapter 41 describes her wretchedness. The key phrases are: 'she was conquered. . . . Her pride was indeed brought low. . . . She hated herself now.'

Worse is to follow: she has to watch Troy kiss the dead Fanny. Her reaction might have been one of loathing, of revulsion, of horror. It is none of these. A wild jealousy overwhelms her; with all her being she still wants him:

> 'I love you better than she did: kiss me too, Frank – kiss me! *You will, Frank, kiss me too!*' (chapter 43)

Quite what Bathsheba went through that night alone in the empty hollow Hardy, perhaps surprisingly, never tells us. But we do know that she meets her despair with fierce resolution (perhaps this is part of her vanity), refusing to run away and advising Liddy:

> 'If ever you marry . . . you'll find yourself in a fearful situation; but mind this, don't you flinch. Stand your ground, and be cut to pieces!' (chapter 44)

Shattered by her experiences of that night with the coffin she 'drew into herself'. Yet she is a survivor, not a contractor-out. Her mood is not one of despair or hysteria or self-pity, but of 'quietude which was not precisely peacefulness'. And she keeps the farm going, although eventually only through Oak.

She agrees to promise to marry Boldwood because, as she tells Gabriel:

> 'I believe that if I don't give my word, he'll go out of his mind.' (chapter 51)

Also because:

> 'I cannot get off my conscience that I once seriously injured him in sheer idleness.' (chapter 51)

She does not love him. Indeed she has acquired a tragic view of love as

> 'an utterly bygone, sorry, worn-out, miserable thing with me.'
> (chapter 51)

Troy's death is the culmination of her suffering. She meets it with an heroic dignity that is the most striking and moving moment of her transformation from the lively, teasing girl we first saw. That she insisted on tending the body herself, even defying the law in so doing, is eloquent testimony to her love for Troy, her powers of self-command and her strength of character. The doctor finds her action awesome:

> 'Gracious heaven – this mere girl! She must have the nerve of a stoic!'
> (chapter 54)

Her recovery takes time. It is a revival of her old self-regard that first gives us a clue to a renewal of vigour – and the unconscious stirring of her love for Gabriel:

> It broke upon her at length as a great pain that her last old disciple was about to forsake her and flee. (chapter 56)

The full realisation of that love and its final consummation are related quietly and without effort. It is appropriate to the story and its themes, and Hardy does not waste time either elaborating or justifying its growth. It is made to seem as natural and inevitable as the healing of a wound.

Bathsheba is not in any way a complex creation. There are no mysteries to her, no puzzling depths or inconsistencies, no subtleties. Yet she is convincingly and powerfully put before us. Betrayed by a streak of vanity (which is the other side of the coin to her independent, confident spirit), she has to pay a heavy price, perhaps not wholly undeserved yet more than most of us have to face for our own shortcomings. She accepts her own responsibility for what happens to her, and this honesty, together with her dignity at her crisis, earn our respect and make us rejoice when she achieves a final calm of happiness.

Oak

His name obviously tells us a lot: oak is tough, durable, can be put to all sorts of uses and has been part of the English landscape since man began to farm. It grows slowly and sends its roots deep.

This account of Oak will be brief; he really needs little commentary to reveal his personality – it is there for all to see: honest and open. (We have already considered his role as a shepherd, a master of his craft, someone vital to the welfare of the community.)

The story opens with a lengthy portrait of Gabriel. In this the insistent emphasis is on his middle position, his avoidance of extremes. Morally he occupies the 'vast middle space' which keeps clear of religious fervour on the one hand, notorious misconduct on the other. His features are manly but have not yet lost 'relics of the boy'. He is neither assertive nor timid, but shows a 'quiet modesty'. He is not over-intellectual nor over-impulsive.

Later, this emphasis on balanced moderation is complemented by a description of his 'quiet energy'. He is capable of thinking and acting quickly but 'his special power, morally, physically and mentally, was static'. So while we see him responding swiftly in crisis moments, his characteristic stance is that of the patient watcher, one who bides his time.

One expects consistency from such a person – and we get it. And restraint. And a self-denying loyalty – he is even to irritate Bathsheba by the undeviating firmness with which he keeps his early resolution: 'Very well . . . . Then I'll ask you no more.'

Well, this is all very admirable. The qualities in Oak are summed up by one admirer, Lascelles Abercrombie, in his book *Thomas Hardy*.

> The steadfast lover, so faithful that personal disappointment is of no account matched with the welfare of the beloved, is the natural flowering here of 'plain heroic magnitude of mind'; of a life whose whole conduct is simple unquestioning patience, a tolerant fortitude deeply rooted in the earth.

The trouble is that all this could be pretty dull. It is always difficult for a writer to create interest in a character who is essentially good and honest and consistent. Irresponsible or wicked characters tend to be much more fun, more fascinating. Integrity and self-restraint, patience and modesty are not very exciting qualities, however valuable.

It is completely a matter of opinion whether the reader finds Gabriel attractive or boring. If you find him a bit too loyal and decent, a touch tame and unsatisfying – well, you won't be the only one. Here, for example, is an uneasiness felt by George Wing in his book *Hardy* (he links Oak with other similar Hardy characters):

> Such characters are male, but curiously unmasculine men: not sexually perverted, but lacking in aggressiveness: in sex-conflict they are out-manœuvred, and their attractive women are often disappointed by their passive chivalry: a little more caddishness and assertiveness at opportune moments would have paid dividends. They are too honourable, too self-effacing, too long-suffering.

However, there are perhaps at least two considerations that may redeem Gabriel from the charge of boring the reader. The first is his role in the story as a whole, where he is set against Troy and Boldwood. James Gibson, the editor of the Macmillan Students' Hardy edition of *Far from the Madding Crowd*, summarises the point usefully in his introduction:

> The superficial Troy and the deeply emotional and obsessive Boldwood, both potentially destructive, represent extremes, and it is for Gabriel, the preserver and creator, to provide the balance.

Like Bathsheba, we may at first acquaintance not be very struck by Gabriel. However, later, when we have seen what damage can be done by violent or irresponsible characters, the suffering this can cause, we begin to appreciate the solid worth of someone like Oak. By himself then he can seem a touch drab; put to the test, seen in contrast to others, given the time to prove his value, he has claims on our admiration.

The second reason he can seem attractive is to do with his personality in itself. The very first sentence of the novel describes how his smile lights up his whole face. We may tend to forget this smile, but we should not underrate Gabriel's sheer good nature. He does nothing mean, nothing petty; he never moans or wraps himself moodily in his own frustration. He is easy-going, a good companion, adapts instinctively to other people. This quality is perhaps best expressed in the scene in the malthouse where he does not fuss about the ash falling in the God-forgive-me mug or the grit in Mark Clark's bacon. Gabriel was once a man of property with bright prospects; but he shows no self-consciousness or resentment when in the company of humbler folk. Right at the end of the story his warm sympathy for the men on the farm (when he might have kept his distance as befitting his new-found status) is shown again when he invites the Weatherbury band 'to have something to eat and drink wi' me and my wife'.

Troy

Although Troy is glimpsed quite early in the story Hardy does not give us any substantial account of him until chapter 25, which is wholly devoted to the sergeant's description. Oak and Boldwood are also presented by a static portrait: Hardy, as it were, stops the action running, the sequence of the story, and holds one frame so that our attention is concentrated on a single character.

Do you think this to be an effective way of doing things? It can be felt rather obvious as a technique, too deliberate and heavy-handed. Also this is not really the way in which we consider people we actually know.

On the other hand, a novel is not life itself and there may be something to be said for pausing in this way, having a gathering-point in which the various threads that make up a personality are drawn together to give a definitive portrait.

In the case of Troy, the second paragraph of his portrait is of particular importance; part of it reads:

> He was a man to whom memories were an encumbrance, and anticipations a superfluity. Simply feeling, considering, and caring for what was before his eyes, he was vulnerable only in the present. . . . With him the past was yesterday; the future, tomorrow; never, the day after.

So he lives for the present, takes life as it comes:

> His activities . . . never being based upon any original choice of foundation or direction, they were exercised on whatever object chance might place in their way.

A farmer can't work like this: he has to think and plan for the farming year. So Troy is immediately established as the antithesis of all that Oak represents. He is irresponsible and impulsive but not vicious in an ugly way, although he certainly treats women in a cavalier, even brutal, manner; but he also flatters them and claims that in dealing with them 'the only alternative to flattery was cursing and swearing'. He is very good at flattery being 'exceptionally well educated for a common soldier'. He speaks 'fluently and unceasingly'. In a crude modern phrase he has 'the gift of the gab'.

Whether the pages of analysis in this chapter make him out as anything more than an attractive but slippery womaniser is doubtful. It has been said that Hardy was not very convincing in creating this type of man (who is in many respects repeated in Alec d'Urberville in *Tess of the d'Urbervilles*). David Cecil, for example, in his book *Hardy the Novelist* has this to say:

> Sergeant Troy in *Far from the Madding Crowd* is the old, typical figure of the dashing, inconstant soldier with a love in every town, who kisses and rides away.

Yet is this really fair? Surely Cecil ignores Troy's devotion to Fanny.

Another critic, George Wing, in *Hardy*, while agreeing that Troy is 'selfish, indulgent, limitedly promiscuous . . . unthinking', points out:

Yet, after all, Bathsheba damaged his life almost as much as he damaged hers. He was prepared to stand by Fanny Robin. He was prepared to marry her. It was Fanny's wretched ill-luck that attendant circumstances were in such mocking contrast: as Troy waited in vain in All Saints Church, there was giggling from the congregation of women and girls and chuckles from toothless old almsmen, but in his courtship of Bathsheba there were chivalrous peacock displays of sword-drill and romantic meetings in the hay-meads. There was a curious warmth in the shallowness of the dandy's heart, and an unexpected fidelity in his fickleness.

He is also, Wing notes, 'what so many of Hardy's heroes are not, aggressively masculine'. Finally this critic points out that in Troy's somewhat melodramatic kissing of the dead Fanny and in 'the gross pretentious headstone, the futile bundle of bulbs' with which he tries to atone for his sense of guilt over the girl's death, there is something pathetic, sharply observed and moving.

So it may be insensitive to see Troy as simply a stock-type 'love 'em and leave 'em' villain. His presentation is arguably energetic, distinctive and not just two-dimensional. You must make up your own mind how convincing he seems.

Boldwood

The 'portrait' of Boldwood that has been already mentioned comes in chapter 18. A key passage runs:

> his was not an ordinary nature. That stillness, which struck casual observers more than anything else in his character and habit, and seemed so precisely like the rest of inanition, may have been the perfect balance of enormous antagonistic forces – positives and negatives in fine adjustment. His equilibrium disturbed, he was in extremity at once. If an emotion possessed him, it ruled him. (chapter 18)

Appearing a man of exceptional calm and control, he is in fact in a state of balanced tension – and once that balance is disturbed then he is lost. He is also a very serious-minded person:

> He had no light and careless touches. . . He saw no absurd sides to the follies of life. (chapter 18)

This combination is particularly dangerous. He is utterly different from Troy, who can essentially shrug off disaster and is frivolous, light-weight where Boldwood is heavily solid. There is a power to the man, who is described as a 'dark and silent shape', or like a volcanic mass whose outward stillness conceals a 'hotbed of tropic intensity'. Once that hotbed surges upwards nothing can arrest or divert it.

The presentation of Boldwood is particularly firm in its outline and convincing in its mass. A man of marked reserve and dignity, he is reduced to a desperation of love that strips him of both these qualities:

> 'O Bathsheba - have pity upon me! . . . God's sake, yes - I am come to that low, lowest stage - to ask a woman for pity! . . . Now the people will sneer at me - the very hills and sky seem to laugh at me till I blush shamefully for my folly. I have lost my respect, my good name, my standing - lost it, never to get it again.' (chapter 31)

He has to endure Troy's 'low gurgle of derisive laughter'; the bitter self-awareness that

> 'I am weak and foolish, and I don't know what, and I can't fend off my miserable grief!' (chapter 38)

The strength of his obsession is revealed in the items of jewellery labelled 'Bathsheba Boldwood', 'pathetic evidences of a mind crazed with care and love'.

The Introduction to the Macmillan Students' Hardy summarises the creation of Boldwood as, 'a masterly study, a minor tragedy in itself and a moving psychological analysis'. His presence throws a shadow across the landscape and even when he is removed from the scene the playfulness and innocence of the novel's opening can never be recaptured.

Workfolk

We always think of them as a group: supping from the 'God-forgive-me' mug in Warren's malthouse, queuing for their wages, clustered round Cain Ball to hear the news from Bath, snoring drunkenly in the barn, gossiping in the dark outside Boldwood's house, forming the band for Bathsheba's and Gabriel's wedding. True, Joseph Poorgrass is solely responsible for Fanny's coffin being late; but this is an isolated and exceptional moment. True also that they have their own idiosyncrasies: Henry Fray insisting on 'H-e-n-e-r-y', Joseph with his blushes, Andrew Randle his stammer, Laban Tall bullied by his wife. Yet these traits are only swift, comic touches, little more than the distinctive make-up worn by each circus-clown. These people achieve their identity as a group rather than as individuals.

That identity is essentially a comic one; there is a clownish side to it. However, we would be very wrong to think of the rustics as simply a comic act, a balance to, and diversion from, the passionate and tragic concerns of the principal performers.

Earlier we saw how Hardy resented the patronising view of a farm-labourer as a country clown, a 'Hodge'. So we would not expect him to take this attitude in his own writing. He enjoys their clumsiness and naivety, yes; he does not suggest that they are heroic or remarkable people. However, he also makes it clear that they have their own admirable qualities.

Inside the malthouse with its courteous friendliness – 'Come in, shepherd; sure ye be welcome, though we don't know yer name' – the conversation is that of a closely knit community who have known each other all their working lives, whose backgrounds and ancestry are common knowledge: the maltster tells Oak:

> 'Knowed yer grandfather for years and years! . . . knowed yer grandmother.' (chapter 8)

Even though they may make fun of some of their number they are essentially sympathetic and understanding:

> ''Tis a' awkward gift for a man, poor soul,' said the maltster. 'And ye have suffered from it a long time, we know.' (chapter 8)

That last phrase 'we know' says a lot: everyone does know about Joseph Poorgrass's blushing, everyone is ready to console and sympathise. There is a great sense of comradeship and togetherness, however clumsy or comical this may be.

Their life may be a hard one but their usual attitude seems to be to accept things as they come. They don't question the rightness or justice of the world or their place in it – except for an occasional grumble such as that from Henery Fray, bitter that he has not been appointed bailiff:

> 'There, 'twas to be, I suppose. Your lot is your lot, and scripture is nothing; for if you do good you don't get rewarded according to your works, but be cheated in some way out of your recompense.' (chapter 15)

However, Henery's somewhat blasphemous outburst meets with a rebuke:

> 'No, no; I don't agree with 'ee there,' said Mark Clark. 'God's a perfect gentleman in that respect.' (chapter 15)

The idea of God as a fair-minded country squire raises a smile, but it does show the labourers' conviction that they ought to be grateful for God's mercies. This is echoed in Joseph's later remark about feeling 'deep cheerfulness' for a 'happy providence'.

Basically contented and uncritical, the workfolk are, however, also shrewdly observant. They frequently comment on the behaviour of the main characters – and they don't miss much:

> 'What a fool she must have been ever to have had anything to do with the man! She is so self-willed and independent too, that one is more minded to say it serves her right than pity her.' (chapter 53)

In their commonsensical, perceptive remarks about the goings-on of their employers the farmhands form a sort of 'chorus' in the old sense of this word, one derived from Greek tragedy. In these plays an anonymous group enter from time to time during the action to express their dismay at what they sense to be the foolishness or disastrous nature of whatever the main characters are up to. The Greek chorus link the central events of tragedy to the fears and forebodings of ordinary people. Their fate is ultimately connected to that of the main characters, who, being rulers or influential persons in the city-state, control the lives of their subjects. This is also true of Hardy's rustics: if their employers neglect the farms, as a result of upheavals in their private lives, then the whole community will suffer.

For finally these simple folk are representatives of the steady pattern of life that the story celebrates; they are directly associated with qualities of endurance and fitness that, as we have seen, are located in the barn:

> So the barn was natural to the shearers; and the shearers were in harmony with the barn. (chapter 22)

Hardy regards them with a countryman's affection, a love that understands and accepts foolishness and simplicity.

4.3 STYLE

'Style' is a difficult term; it means so many different things. A writer's style has been defined as being 'the man himself' – that is to say, the expression of his whole personality, not simply a technical skill acquired like that of a mechanic. 'Style' implies the whole character of a writer's work: it cannot finally be separated from his subject matter, his sympathies, his ideas and themes.

Nevertheless, when applied to a writer, style is usually thought of in the first instance as describing the way he handles language, his voice as it were. Each one of us has a distinctive tone of voice by which we can be recognised, and the same is true of a good writer: he has his individual 'voice'. Hardy's use of language is utterly his own, instantly recognisable. What are its characteristics in *Far from the Madding Crowd?*

Dialogue

A great deal of the novel is related in a plain, vigorous narrative style. Quotation can't really illustrate this. Just read any passage where the story has a good pace to it and there are no interruptions for discussion or comment. For example, chapters 34, 35 and 36.

Notice that in chapter 34 there is a lot of dialogue. Although Hardy's dialogue can be unconvincing, here it is briskly effective; the exchanges are often very crisp. For example:

> 'Come to that, is it!' murmured Boldwood, uneasily.
> 'You promised silence,' said Troy.
> 'I promise again.'
> Troy stepped forward.
> 'Frank, dearest, is that you?' The tones were Bathsheba's.
> 'O God!' said Boldwood.
> 'Yes,' said Troy to her.
> 'How late you are,' she continued tenderly.

Or:

> 'A moment,' he gasped. 'You are injuring her you love!'
> 'Well, what do you mean?' said the farmer.
> 'Give me breath,' said Troy.
> Boldwood loosened his hand, saying, 'By Heaven, I've a mind to kill you!'
> 'And ruin her.'
> 'Save her.'
> 'Oh, how can she be saved now, unless I marry her?'

Even in this exchange there is one phrase that can seem a touch melodramatic, theatrical rather than the actual expression a person might use in such a situation:

> 'You are injuring her you love!'

Later in this chapter Boldwood is to exclaim:

> 'You juggler of Satan! You black hound! But I'll punish you yet; mark me, I'll punish you yet!'

These phrases are getting dangerously close to melodrama: it would be easy to send them up, very difficult for an actor to say them with a straight face if the dialogue were to be used for an adaptation of the novel for acting.

However, having said this, the slightly unfortunate effect is probably noticeable only if we pause, take the dialogue out from its context and look at it unsympathetically. Put it back in its violent context and the power of the whole confrontation between Boldwood and Troy can be felt to charge the phrase with an impetus that restores its appropriate strength.

A type of dialogue that has been admired in the novel is that used by the workfolk. Hardy knew his local dialect intimately and particularly admired the work of a Dorset poet, William Barnes, who wrote his poems in dialect. There is a kind of poetry in the speech Hardy gives to his rustics, full of metaphor and rich phrasing:

> – And so I used to eat a lot of salt fish afore going, and then by the time I got there I were as dry as a lime-basket – so thorough dry that ale would slip down – ah, 'twould slip down sweet! Happy times! Such lovely drunks as I used to have at that house! (chapter 8)

'Lovely drunks' –what a superb phrase. One other speech:

> Heh-heh! well, I wish to noise nothing abroad – nothing at all. . . . But we be born to things – that's true. Yet I would rather my trifle be hid; though, perhaps, a high nater is a little high, and at my birth all things were possible to my Maker, and he may have begrudged no gifts. (chapter 33)

Always alive and with its own distinctively sturdy character, this country speech is one of the delights of the novel. Personality always thrusts out of the dialogue: we don't just read it, we hear it and are vividly aware of the speaker:

> I saw our mistress . . . and a sojer, walking along. And bymeby they got closer and closer, and then they went arm-in-crook, like courting complete – hok-hok! like courting complete – hok! – courting complete. (chapter 33)

There is an unflagging vitality. Hardy is particularly confident and vivacious in his writing here - so different from the somewhat crabbed, self-conscious literariness we noted earlier. There is no sense of effort or strain, but a sure touch, deft and joyous.

However, some critics have felt that Hardy does lay on the dialect, that is, he makes the rustics rather more colourful, more rich in vocabulary and phrasing than these would have been among actual nineteenth-century farmhands. This is probably true - but so what? Would the novel really be improved in any way if the workfolk's turn of speech were less lively and distinctive?

Observed detail

Close observation of detail is evident throughout the novel. The second chapter opens with an account of the wind:

> The hill was covered on its northern side by an ancient and decaying plantation of beeches, whose upper verge formed a line over the crest, fringing its arched curve against the sky, like a man. To-night these trees sheltered the southern slope from the keenest blasts, which smote the wood and floundered through it with a sound as of grumbling, or gushed over its crowning boughs in a weakened moan. The dry leaves in the ditch simmered and boiled in the same breezes, a tongue of air occasionally ferreting out a few, and sending them spinning across the grass.

The last sentence here is vibrant with touches that are both exact in their observation and alive with inventive metaphors. Notice how well the verbs are used: 'simmered and boiled', 'ferreting'. In the previous sentence 'floundered and gushed' are also so effective. Verbs are the sinews of a sentence: a good writer will always get a high work-rate out of them - not just pile on adjectives.

In the following paragraph the different sounds of the wind through grass are noted with a keenness of ear that is quite remarkable:

> The thin grasses, more or less coating the hill, were touched by the wind in breezes of differing natures - one rubbing the blades heavily, another raking them piercingly, another brushing them like a soft broom.

In the next paragraph Hardy's sight is shown to be as acute as his hearing:

> A difference of colour in the stars - oftener read of than seen in England - was really perceptible here. The sovereign brilliancy of

Sirius pierced the eye with a steely glitter, the star called Capella was yellow, Aldebaran and Betelgueux shone with a fiery red.

Throughout these descriptions the movement of the prose is energetic, the structure of the sentences fluent and forward-moving. The effects are not held up by any oddities of syntax (the way sentences are built up) or ponderousness in vocabulary. Again, the touch is sure, the writing instinct with life.

The description of the storm at the centre of the novel is famous and often quoted. You can find abundant examples here of the excellences we have detected in the second chapter. The description of the swamp in chapter 44 is another fine passage with the 'beautiful yellowing ferns with their feathery arms'; the 'morning mist . . . a fulsome yet magnificent silvery veil, full of light from the sun, yet semi-opaque'; the fungi 'with stems like macaroni'. Later in this chapter there is a lovely detail noted with the sheep drinking: 'the water dribbling from their lips in silver threads'.

Always the descriptive passages are expressive of the mood of the story, the experience of the characters. They are not simply decorative but resonant. So the winds and stars image Gabriel's harmony with natural forces; the storm's destructive power recalls the ravages Troy is effecting in the settled calm of farming life; the hollow where Troy displays his swordsmanship is secret and sensuous; the malignancy of the swamp threatens and frightens in a nightmarish sequel to the horror of the dead child in the coffin.

Lighting effects

A very distinctive trait of Hardy's writing is the use of strong lighting: his imagination time and again conceives an episode in terms of light and darkness emphatically rendered. Dramatic effects are realised with a particular visual intensity. They are in part responsible for an experience of reading Hardy's novels that has often been noted: we tend to remember them as a succession of vividly individual scenes rather than as a broad sweep of narrative.

As *Far from the Madding Crowd* develops we are given a series of night scenes, each with its own quality and character. The blaze at the ricks creates theatrical highlights:

His weary face now began to be painted over with a rich orange glow, and the whole front of his smock-front and gaiters was covered with a dancing shadow pattern of thorn-twigs – the light reaching him through a leafless intervening hedge – and the metallic curve of his sheep-crook shone silver-bright in the same abounding rays. (chapter 6)

The kiln in the malthouse is angled like stage footlights: its ruddy glow

shone over the floor with the streaming horizontality of the setting sun, and threw upwards the shadows of all facial irregularities in those assembled around. (chapter 8)

This is a very different lighting effect from that created by the rick fire. An even sharper difference is seen in the next night episode, that outside Troy's barracks – there is no light source: a 'vast arch of cloud' obscures the sky, and

If anything could be darker than the sky, it was the wall, and if anything could be gloomier than the wall it was the river beneath. (chapter 11)

A rich tranquillity – but yet with an ominously dead quality about it – illumines the meeting between Bathsheba and Boldwood after the shearing-supper. The whole scene is very reminiscent of the tonal effects of those Dutch paintings for which Hardy had a particular fondness:

It was still the beaming time of evening, though night was stealthily making itself visible low down upon the ground, the western lines of light raking the earth without alighting upon it to any extent, or illuminating the dead levels at all. The sun had crept round the tree as a last effort before death, and then began to sink, the shearers' lower parts becoming steeped in browning twilight, whilst their heads and shoulders were still enjoying day. (chapter 23)

As a last example of these evocative night scenes let us take Bathsheba's first meeting with Troy where the lighting effect is again devised with precision. This time there is a weirdness to the theatrical quality of the lighting:

He too stooped, and the lantern standing on the ground betwixt them threw the gleam from its open side among the fir-tree needles and the blades of a long damp grass with the effect of a large glow-worm. It radiated upwards into their faces, and sent over half the plantation gigantic shadows of both man and woman, each dusky shape becoming distorted and mangled upon the tree-trunks till it wasted to nothing. (chapter 24)

No other English novelist so consistently exhibits this visual range in terms of light. Always there is a sense of a scenic effect such as a theatre lighting consultant might devise. Also there is a poetic intensity in the presentation of the scene: it glows or throbs or lours in accord with the passions enacted 'on stage'.

We began this section on 'Style' by noting that it was a difficult term, not some kind of trick of the trade, not merely a technical skill that can be mastered by study like a foreign language, but an expression of the writer's whole personality. Deliberate care in handling words and a conscious development of the art of constructing a novel do of course come into it; but invention and instinct are the most important and vital factors.

Poetic resonance

The heading is meant to indicate the way in which so many of Hardy's descriptions of small incidents seem to have a power of suggestiveness, an elusive inner stillness that radiates out from whatever is being presented to the reader. In this we can see Hardy's poetic sensibility – he is a major poet, of course, as well as a major novelist. Some examples will help to make clearer this quality of 'poetic resonance'.

Think of Bathsheba on top of that waggon with the looking-glass 'in which she proceeded to survey herself attentively. She parted her lips and smiled.' Then see her on the hayrick in the storm: 'The soft and continual shimmer of the dying lightning showed a marble face high against the black sky'. Then when Troy comes to claim her: 'sunk down on the lowest stair, her mouth blue and dry, and her dark eyes fixed vacantly upon him'. Each moment 'fixes' her in the sense that a developed negative is 'fixed'; each is a picture in sharp focus; each is exposed in such a way as to sum up her mood and situation with a visual eloquence which, while centring on her in a particular pose at a particular moment, somehow also suggests a wider image, moving and memorable: the essential woman.

This kind of image is presented throughout the novel. Think of Fanny when Gabriel meets her: 'the young girl remained motionless by the tree'; or of Troy at an upper window of the farmhouse: 'The soldier turned a little towards the east, and the sun kindled his scarlet coat to an orange glow.'

All these forceful and concentrated portrayals are consistent with Hardy's narrative art as a whole: his declared preference for the unusual and the striking; the sequence of dramatic incidents; the firm outlines with which his characters are drawn. The treatment of detail and the treatment of the whole need to be set in the same key if the novel is to harmonise. This is so in *Far from the Madding Crowd*: in every aspect of the work, Hardy's style is vigorous, dramatic and poetic.

5 EXAMINATION

OF A

SPECIMEN PASSAGE

The extract chosen for study comes from the first chapter of the novel:

The girl on the summit of the load sat motionless, surrounded by tables and chairs with their legs upwards, backed by an oak settle, and ornamented in front by pots of geraniums, myrtles, and cactuses, together with a caged canary – all probably from the windows of the house just vacated. There was also a cat in a willow basket, from the partly-opened lid of which she gazed with half-closed eyes, and affectionately surveyed the small birds around.

The handsome girl waited for some time idly in her place, and the only sound heard in the stillness was the hopping of the canary up and down the perches of its prison. Then she looked attentively downwards. It was not at the bird, nor at the cat; it was at an oblong package tied in paper, and lying between them. She turned her head to learn if the waggoner were coming. He was not yet in sight; and her eyes crept back to the package, her thoughts seeming to run upon what was inside it. At length she drew the article into her lap, and untied the paper covering; a small swing looking-glass was disclosed, in which she proceeded to survey herself attentively. She parted her lips and smiled.

It was a fine morning, and the sun lighted up to a scarlet glow the crimson jacket she wore, and painted a soft lustre upon her bright face and dark hair. The myrtles, geraniums, and cactuses packed around her were fresh and green, and at such a leafless season they invested the whole concern of horses, waggon, furniture, and girl with a peculiar vernal charm. What possessed her to indulge in such a performance in the sight of the sparrows, blackbirds, and unperceived farmer who were alone its spectators, – whether the smile began as a factitious one, to test her capacity in that art, – nobody knows; it ended certainly in a real smile.

She blushed at herself, and seeing her reflection blush, blushed the more.

The change from the customary spot and necessary occasion of such an act – from the dressing hour in a bedroom to a time of travelling out of doors – lent to the idle deed a novelty it did not intrinsically possess. The picture was a delicate one. Woman's prescriptive infirmity had stalked into the sunlight, which had clothed it in the freshness of an originality. A cynical inference was irresistible by Gabriel Oak as he regarded the scene, generous though he fain would have been. There was no necessity whatever for looking in the glass. She did not adjust her hat, or pat her hair, or press a dimple into shape, or do one thing to signify that any such intention had been her motive in taking up the glass. She simply observed herself as a fair product of Nature in the feminine kind, her thoughts seeming to glide into far-off though likely dramas in which men would play a part – vistas of probable triumphs – the smiles being of a phase suggesting that hearts were imagined as lost and won. Still, this was but conjecture, and the whole series of actions was so idly put forth as to make it rash to assert that intention had any part in them at all.

The waggoner's steps were heard returning. She put the glass in the paper, and the whole again into its place.

(New Wessex Edition, Bayley, 1975, pages 43–4)

This is the first time we see Bathsheba. What kinds of effect does the description have on the reader?

The tone of the first paragraph is one of relaxed observation, 'casually glancing over the hedge', in keeping with the actual watcher, Gabriel Oak. Simply, without elaborate detail, the girl's situation (rather than the girl herself) is first seen, the confusion of her setting with its faintly comic air: 'tables and chairs with their legs upwards'. The simplicity of the objects in the waggon, the care with which the flowers and cactuses, canary and cat have been tucked in among them, suggest both the humble social status of their owner and her displacement – both important to the opening stages of the novel. They also suggest something about her personality – what, . . . would you say? And what about the cat? How do you interpret 'affectionately'? (Are cats usually kind to birds?)

In the second paragraph we look at the girl. First, a distinctive detail: the only sound is the movement of the canary in its cage. This emphasises the isolated stillness of the scene and also indirectly reminds us of Gabriel's hidden, silent watchfulness. The moment is held in time, but not in any romantic haze. It is all acutely and solidly there in front of us. In the second short sentence the pace quickens with a gesture: 'she looked attentively downwards'. The structure of the next phrase, 'it was not at the bird, nor at the cat', teases us with its negative (what *was* she looking at then?) It also gives a forward impulse: we want to learn what she is up to. The paragraph is rounded off with a brief, revealing – rather charming – conclusion: 'She parted her lips and smiled'.

The third paragraph introduces – so characteristically of Hardy – a lighting effect: a fine morning, the sun. All these effects of light give something special to both the girl and her whole context. Surely we have two aspects of her character suggested in the 'scarlet glow' and the 'soft lustre'? (What aspects might these be?) The sense of open freshness and vitality which light up the opening of the novel (for it starts with Gabriel's smile) is here also. This warmth of lighting is to contrast dramatically with the constant night scenes, their vivid lanterns, fires and lightning, which are to be seen in the story's later developments.

Then the flowers are referred to again with their 'vernal charm'. This is an example of Hardy's tendency to use words derived from Latin: 'vernal' rather than, say, 'spring'. The flowers contrast vividly with Bathsheba's crimson jacket and dark hair – a contrast which again suggests further aspects of her personality.

The sentence beginning, 'What possessed her . . .' shifts the tone slightly. Hardy is now not just observing; he is speculating – in a cheating kind of way. When he says that 'nobody knows' what was going through her mind, he is playing a kind of game with the reader. Hardy could perfectly well have told us what she was thinking, as he is to do frequently later on. But at this stage he likes to keep us at a distance, to tease us with an 'I wonder what on earth she was up to' approach. This fits in with Gabriel's puzzlement (he does *not* know what her motives are) and with the early stages of the story: it is too soon yet for us to be intimate with Bathsheba.

The fourth paragraph continues this shift. There is no more precise observation at all; instead Hardy comments. First, on the oddness of a woman taking out a looking-glass in this way; and second, on the fact that women are naturally vain. Again we have a Latinate vocabulary in 'prescriptive infirmity', rather a mouthful of a phrase which means something like 'built-in weakness'. Whether you find Hardy's remark about women in general to be true or false, shrewd or cynical, is up to you.

When, in the last sentence of this paragraph he says, 'Still, this was but conjecture . . .' we are faced with something of a puzzle: *whose* conjecture (guess)? Hardy's? Gabriel's? Ours? Whatever the answer, the effect of this comment is to leave us still 'outside' Bathsheba as it were, still trying to work out what she was up to.

Then in a swift, almost staccato phrase, we, like Bathsheba, are startled out of leisurely thoughts by the sound of the waggoner's returning steps. Action takes over from speculation; the story is under way again.

*   *   *

So what do we have in this passage?

A sharply focused scene with the kind of distinctive oddness that we meet so often in Hardy. The manner and tone is lightly amusing; the scene is being observed from the viewpoint of an intrigued, hidden bystander. So there is little exposition; that is, authoritative statements telling us what the character is feeling. Instead, we are provocatively teased in a way that fits in with the mood of the novel's opening.

In the first three paragraphs and in the last the observation is sharp, the vocabulary and rhythms are clean, sparse, vigorous. In the fourth paragraph we are invited to mull over the scene. Here the vocabulary tends to be more ponderous. What, for example, has been gained by the substitution of the rather awkward and coy phrase 'a fair product of Nature in the feminine kind' for the simple 'handsome girl' of the second paragraph?

Do you think the point of view in this passage is essentially critical – a vain young missie? Or admiring – what an attractive young girl? Or only neutral, leaving all judgement to the reader (and Gabriel)? In considering any passage from a novel it is usually worthwhile trying to detect what relationship the writer is establishing with his characters, how he is seeing them, how he invites the reader to see them.

6 CRITICAL RECEPTION

Far from the Madding Crowd has been consistently admired; only a few critics have been unsympathetic. It represents a kind of watershed in Hardy's writing. The novels which came before it were nearly all uneven in quality or hesitant in some way, showing promise, but flawed in structure or balance. The later novels, while mostly more ambitious in their range, were more sombre in their view of life: the joyousness and serene conclusion of *Far from the Madding Crowd* were never to be repeated.

While the novel may not quite be a masterpiece of the same order of achievement of works such as *The Mayor of Casterbridge* or *Tess of the d'Urbervilles*, it is very assured. It is not without faults and clearly has its limitations. But it has attracted far more admiration and affection than hostility or disparagement.

Even before all the instalments had been published in the *Cornhill Magazine* it was being widely acclaimed. When it was published in book form in 1874 the critics were nearly unanimous in finding it a powerful story. Reviews in *The Times* and *The Manchester Guardian* admired in particular the firmness of the presentation of the characters. Among the spate of favourable comment in literary periodicals there was some criticism of the dialogue of the 'rustics' which was thought to be 'over written'; that is, more amusing or poetic or rich in phrasing than anything a country person would actually say.

Only the novelist Henry James was wholly hostile – as has been noted earlier in this commentary (p. 60). Nevertheless, for the rest of the nineteenth century there was a tendency for some critics to be rather patronising in their attitude, telling Hardy that his real talent was for writing entertainingly about simple country people in a social backwater.

Twentieth-century opinion about Hardy's general achievement has not been unanimous. For instance, a very influential critic on the inter-war period, F. R. Leavis did not consider Hardy very seriously, placing him quite outside what he saw as the mainstream or 'Great Tradition', as he called it, of the English novel. He considered Hardy a limited, minor writer without the intellectual stature or grasp of the contemporary world shown by novelists such as George Eliot, Henry James or D. H. Lawrence. Yet Lawrence himself was a great admirer of Hardy's work.

More recent critics have made higher claims for Hardy, and he is generally now thought of as a major novelist with a unique imaginative power.

In *Hardy the Novelist*, which at the time of its publication in 1943 was very highly praised as 'a superb and penetrating piece of criticism' and 'a noble tribute to a novelist whose greatness even yet . . . is not enough understood', Lord David Cecil eloquently expressed his love of, and high regard for, Hardy. Among other qualities he praised what he called Hardy's 'visualising faculty' and 'power of visual invention':

> It is not just that he makes us see a scene. He invents scenes which, of their very nature, stir the imagination. Not only does he describe the incident graphically; the incident is itself mysteriously arresting and exciting. *Far from the Madding Crowd*, in particular, is full of such episodes.

However, *Far from the Madding Crowd* is not usually thought of as one of Hardy's major works. For example, George Wing, in his study *Hardy* published in 1963, groups the novels according to the layout of a dartboard as 'outers', 'inners' and 'bulls'. He places *Far from the Madding Crowd* as an 'inner'; that is, a novel of distinctive quality, but not among Hardy's finest, the 'bulls'. His view can be represented by his summary:

> There is good humour and many stretches of sunny pages. It is essentially a sheep and shepherd book, for which one has a deep affection, and the darker work of the main characters is played out against the frolicsomeness of malthouse gatherings, sheep shearings, harvest suppers and Christmas parties.

Douglas Brown in *Thomas Hardy* published in 1954 deals particularly with Hardy's concern for the agricultural life of the Dorset environment. In writing of *Far from the Madding Crowd* Brown comments on the importance of the farming work described in the novel:

> The agricultural context controls the force of the tale. The choral interludes of the fields and the malthouse take their quality from the country rituals and activities they celebrate – the birth of calves and lambs, the seasons of the fair, of harvest, the sheepwashing, the grinding, the incising, the shearing, the hiving. These activities culminate in the intenser activity of emergency: the binding and

covering and thatching of the ricks in the hour of darkness menaced by immense storm.

Although Brown notes an unevenness in the quality of the writing in *Far from the Madding Crowd* he finds the novel as a whole to have a 'special grace'.

Michael Millgate in his *Thomas Hardy: His Career as a Novelist*, published in 1971, is a particularly enthusiastic admirer of *Far from the Madding Crowd*, calling it 'a novel of astonishing confidence', displaying 'extraordinary creative exuberance'. He remarks on 'the excitement and assurance of a writer who has been given his great opportunity'.

So, from its first publication *Far from the Madding Crowd* has been praised and loved. However, it is probably true to say that most early critics were slightly patronising or reserved. It is not until the twentieth century that the novel has been fully appreciated, seen not as a simple country tale, but as a subtly organised and rich work of fiction, both disturbing and joyous.

QUESTIONS AND EXERCISES

The story

1. 'Chance may initiate events but the development of the story owes more to character.' Is this fair comment on *Far from the Madding Crowd*?
2. 'The deaths in *Far from the Madding Crowd* are too convenient and too dramatic to be convincing.' Is this true?
3. In constructing his story, how does Hardy balance tragic incidents with pastoral romance?
4. Explain the importance to the story of any TWO night scenes.

Revision exercises:

a. Make a plan of the events of the sheep-farming year described in *Far from the Madding Crowd*. How important are these in the development of the story?
b. In what ways has Hardy shaped the events of chapters 1–40 to allow for the nine months of Fanny's pregnancy?
c. The novel was first published in magazine instalments: twelve in all. These were of approximately the same length and each contains a dramatic incident. Can you work out which chapters might have corresponded to each instalment? Do your estimates tell you anything about the way the story was constructed?
d. Which events in the story seem to you predictable, which are surprises? When you have worked this out, think about the ways in which the reader's interest in the story is kept alive: Are unexpected developments important here? or not really?

Characters

1. Does Bathsheba deserve what she gets?
2. Is Troy simply the 'villain'?

3. Can you defend Gabriel Oak from the charge of being a boring character who simply bides his time?
4. 'Troy is the only one with energy and drive. All the other main characters in *Far from the Madding Crowd* are, in one way or another, his victims, reacting to his initiatives.' Is this a sound judgement?

Revision exercises:

a. List the ways in which the characters are involved in farm-work. Who has the most involvement? who the least? Does your list suggest anything about Hardy's attitudes towards his characters?
b. Make a list of the times and ways in which Oak comes to Bathsheba's assistance.
c. Imagine you are the casting director for the film of *Far from the Madding Crowd*. Make some notes about the kind of physical characteristics and personal qualities you would look for in the actors to play Oak, Troy and Boldwood and the actress to play Bathsheba.

Other topics

1. 'Hardy's novels are visual novels. It is in his ability to make us 'see' that his greatest strength lies.' (DAVID CECIL). In what ways can this comment be applied to *Far from the Madding Crowd*?
2. *Far from the Madding Crowd* is often praised for being a 'pastoral romance', 'a shepherd's tale', 'a ballad-like story'. Do such phrases really do justice to the achievement of the novel?
3. 'The workfolk in *Far from the Madding Crowd* may not *do* much – but they still contribute a great deal to the novel.' What do they contribute?
4. 'Weatherbury is not simply a location but a way of life; its values determine the success or failure of the people who live there.' Discuss.

Revision exercise:

Take any two strongly visual episodes (as described in Question 1 above); imagine you are a film director and give instructions to your camera crew about the visual qualities in the episodes that you want to emphasise on film.

FURTHER READING

Douglas Brown, *Thomas Hardy* (London: Longmans, Green, 1961). Generally concerned in the first instance with Hardy's commitment to agricultural life in the Dorset environment, Brown does have a few pages directly on *Far from the Madding Crowd*. The whole book is full of interesting insights and is particularly well written.

David Cecil, *Hardy the Novelist* (London: Constable, 1943). Although superseded in some respects, this is still a lively and warm account of Hardy's work in general – one of the first to claim him as a major writer. Lord Cecil does not deal with *Far from the Madding Crowd* in any one part of his book, though there are many references to it.

James Gibson (ed.), *Far from the Madding Crowd* (The Macmillan Students' Hardy) (London: Macmillan, 1975). The Introduction to this edition is a stimulating account of the novel intended for students and making a number of observant comments.

Robert Gittings, *Young Thomas Hardy* (London: Heinemann, 1975). A much admired biography (of which this is the first part) which covers the writing and publication of *Far from the Madding Crowd*, with a lot of revealing and very well-recounted biographical material.

Michael Millgate, *Thomas Hardy: His Career as a Novelist* (London: The Bodley Head, 1971). A generally very perceptive account of Hardy's work, with a refreshingly enthusiastic survey of *Far from the Madding Crowd*, which Millgate sees as a work of 'astonishing confidence'.

Merryn Williams, *A Preface to Hardy* (Preface Books Series) (London: Longman, 1976). A general survey with many references to *Far from the Madding Crowd*, though no specific section on the novel. A very interesting account of Hardy's whole work closely related to his life, background and general thinking.

George Wing, *Hardy* (Edinburgh: Oliver & Boyd, 1963). Grouping Hardy's novels in dartboard terms into 'outers', 'inners' and 'bulls', Wing places *Far from the Madding Crowd* among the 'inners' and gives a well-balanced account of the novel, showing its limitations, but also admiring its qualities.